MODERN COOKING

CREATIVE AMERICAN COOKING
WITH AN INTERNATIONAL FLAVOR

® Landoll, Inc.
Ashland, Ohio 44805
Text and photographs
© 1995 Coombe Books Ltd.
Cover
© 1996 Landoll, Inc.

TABLE OF CONTENTS

Photography by Peter Barry
Designed by Richard Hawke and Claire Leighton
Edited by Jillian Stewart and Kate Cranshaw
Recipes by Judith Ferguson, Lalita Ahmed and
    Carolyn Garner

QUICK
& EASY
COOKING

® Landoll, Inc.
Ashland, Ohio 44805

Contents

Introduction

Many people who do not have much time and energy to spend shopping or preparing meals have resorted to buying 'fast food' in the form of ready-prepared meals and take-aways. Unfortunately, as well as being an expensive way to eat, it does not necessarily guarantee an adequate supply of vitamins, minerals and fibre. For these very reasons, there has been something of a resurgence of home-cooking with an emphasis on quick and easy meals. With this in mind it is essential to know how to prepare food quickly and, just as importantly, what ingredients to use for the minimum of effort. Certain foods such as pasta, salads, fish, shellfish and eggs, are perfectly suited to quick cooking, but it is often the choice of meat which people find difficult. The various cuts best suited to quick cooking are as follows:

Beef - steak and minute steak, mince
Veal - escalopes, calves' liver
Pork - tenderloin (sliced into medallions), mince, steaks, chops, escalopes, liver
Lamb - noisettes, cutlets, leg chops, neck fillet, liver, kidney
Poultry - breast, escalopes, mince, liver
Game - duck breast, venison steak

Obviously, the method of cooking is all important, and you will find that in *Quick and Easy Cooking* there is less baking in the oven and more grilling, pan- and stir-frying and sautéeing. These short methods of cooking are very effective with the cuts of meat and fish already mentioned. Organisation and making the most of the time that you have available is all important. For cooks in a hurry the freezer can be most advantageous, as many people find it easier to do a large amount of cooking when they have the time, freeze it, and buy accompaniments such as fresh fruit and vegetables as required.

When short of time, entertaining can pose a problem. Planning is the key to success here and ease of preparation paramount. Choose one or two dishes, such as a starter (try Quick Liver Paté, Fennel and Orange Croustade or Stuffed Eggs) and a dessert, (such as Crepes, Strawberry Cloud, or Chocolate Brandy Mousse) that can be prepared in advance, even the day before. Dishes that can be part prepared and then frozen are also a boon, but remember to allow sufficient thawing time in your schedule. The main course should be something easy but effective, such as Trout with Chive Sauce, Chicken with Cherries, or Veal Scallopine with Prosciutto. This allows you the maximum time with guests, with the minimum of fuss and effort.

As you can see, successful quick and easy cooking may require a bit of thought at first and perhaps some change to your normal cooking style, but once undertaken this new way of cooking will soon become second nature and the term 'fast food' will have a new meaning in your household.

Spinach and Apple Soup

The two main flavors complement each other perfectly in this hearty soup.

SERVES 4

2 tbsps butter or margarine
1 small onion, minced
2 tbsps all-purpose flour
2½ cups vegetable broth
5 cups spinach, shredded
1 cup unsweetened applesauce
1¼ cups milk
Salt and freshly ground black pepper
Pinch of nutmeg
Lemon juice
Plain yogurt
A little minced parsley

1. Melt the butter in a large saucepan and sauté the onion until soft.

2. Add the flour and cook to a pale straw color.

3. Add the stock slowly, stirring well, and simmer for 10 minutes.

4. Add the spinach and cook until tender.

5. Cool slightly and mix in the applesauce.

6. Place all the ingredients in a liquidizer and blend until smooth.

7. Return to the pan and reheat slowly together with the milk.

8. Add the salt and pepper, nutmeg, and lemon juice to taste.

9. Serve in individual bowls with the yogurt swirled on the top and garnish with minced parsley.

TIME: Preparation takes 15 minutes, cooking takes 15 minutes.

COOK'S TIP: The applesauce can be omitted if not available but it adds an unusual flavor to the soup.

VARIATIONS: If there is no vegetable water available for the broth, a vegetable soup cube can be mixed with 2½ cups of boiling water.

EASY LENTIL SOUP

A good old-fashioned soup which is sure to please all the family.

SERVES 4-6

1 cup split red lentils
2 tbsps butter or margarine
1 medium onion, minced
2 celery stalks, finely diced
2 carrots, finely diced
Grated rind of 1 lemon
5 cups pale-colored vegetable broth
Salt and freshly ground black pepper

1. Sift the lentils and remove any stones. Rinse well.

2. Heat the butter or margarine in a skillet and sauté the onion for 2-3 minutes.

3. Add the diced celery and carrots, and let the vegetables cook on low heat for 5-10 minutes.

4. Stir in the lentils, add the lemon rind, broth, and salt and pepper to taste.

5. Bring to the boil, reduce the heat and simmer for 15-20 minutes or until the vegetables are tender.

6. Blend the soup briefly in a liquidizer; it should not be too smooth.

7. Check the seasoning and reheat gently.

TIME: Preparation takes about 10 minutes, cooking takes 15-20 minutes.

SERVING IDEAS: Sprinkle with cheese and serve with hot toast.

TO FREEZE: Freeze for up to 3 months.

Miso Soup

This delicious soup of Japanese origin makes a nice change for a appetizer.

SERVES 2

1 small onion, grated
¾-inch fresh root ginger, peeled and finely
    chopped
1 clove garlic, crushed
1 tbsp sesame oil
1 carrot, finely sliced
¼ small cauliflower, divided into flowerets
5 cups water
1 large tbsp arame (Japanese seaweed)
¼ cup peas (fresh or frozen)
2 tbsps shoyu (Japanese soy sauce)
1 tbsp miso (soya bean paste)
Black pepper to taste
2 green onions, finely chopped

1. Sauté the onion, ginger, and garlic in the sesame oil for a few minutes.

2. Add the carrot and cauliflower, and gently cook the vegetables for 5 minutes.

3. Add the water, arame, peas, and shoyu. Cook for 15-20 minutes or until the vegetables are soft.

4. Blend the miso to a paste with a little of the soup liquid and add to the soup, but do not allow to boil.

5. Season with freshly ground black pepper to taste.

6. Serve garnished with chopped green onions.

TIME: Preparation takes 15 minutes, cooking takes 20 minutes.

SERVING IDEAS: Serve with hot garlic bread.

VARIATIONS: Substitute other vegetables such as white radish (daikon), turnip, broccoli, snow-peas, or green beans but remember that this soup is mainly a thin broth with a few floating vegetables.

COOK'S TIP: Arame, shoyu, and miso are available from oriental food stores and some health food stores.

CROUTON-STUDDED CRISPY SHRIMP BALLS

These crispy, crouton-coated shrimp balls make an excellent appetizer or snack.

SERVES 4

4 slices white bread
8 ounces white fish fillets
1 cup cooked, shelled shrimp
2 tsps salt
Pepper to taste
2 egg whites
2 slices fresh root ginger, finely chopped
2 tbsps cornstarch
Oil for deep-frying

1. Remove crusts from the bread. Cut each slice into small crouton-sized cubes. Spread out on a large cookie sheet and dry in a hot oven until slightly browned.

2. Chop the fish and shrimp very finely. Mix with the salt, pepper, egg white, ginger, and cornstarch. Blend well.

3. Shape the mixture into 2-inch balls, and roll these over the croutons to coat them.

4. Heat the oil in a deep-fryer. Add the crouton-studded shrimp balls one by one. Turn with a perforated spoon until evenly browned, this takes about 2 minutes. Remove and drain.

5. Return to the oil and cook for a further 1 minute. Drain well on kitchen paper.

TIME: Preparation takes about 15 minutes and cooking takes 3 minutes per batch.

COOK'S TIP: Fry the prawn balls in batches if necessary.

SERVING IDEAS: Serve with a good quality soy sauce, ketchup or chili sauce as dips.

EGGS BAKED IN TARRAGON CREAM

Extremely quick and easy to make, this is a very tasty way of cooking eggs for either a quick snack or an appetizer.

SERVES 4

2 tbsps butter
4 large eggs
1 tbsp chopped fresh tarragon
Salt and pepper
4 tbsps heavy cream

1. Butter 4 individual ovenproof ramekin dishes, and break an egg into each one.

2. In a small bowl, stir the chopped tarragon, and salt and pepper into the cream, and mix well.

3. Spoon 1 tbsp of the cream mixture onto each egg.

4. Put the ramekins onto a cookie sheet and bake in a preheated 350°F oven, for about 6-8 minutes or until set. Serve immediately.

TIME: Preparation takes about 5 minutes, and cooking takes up to 8 minutes.

PREPARATION: Check the eggs during the cooking to see how hard they have become. If you cook them for 8 minutes, they will be very set. If you require a softer yolk, cook them for a shorter time.

SERVING IDEAS: Serve piping hot with buttered toast or crusty French bread.

FENNEL AND ORANGE CROUSTADE

A delicious mixture which is simple to prepare and suitable to serve to company.

SERVES 4

1-inch-thick slices whole-wheat bread
Oil for deep-frying
2 fennel bulbs (reserve any fronds)
4 oranges
1 tbsp olive oil
Pinch salt
Chopped fresh mint to garnish

1. Trim the crusts off the bread and cut into 3-inch squares.

2. Hollow out the centers, leaving evenly-shaped cases.

3. Heat the oil in a deep-fat fryer or large saucepan and deep-fry the bread until golden-brown.

4. Drain the bread well on absorbent kitchen paper, and leave to cool.

5. Trim the fennel bulbs and slice thinly. Place in a mixing bowl.

6. Remove all the peel and white parts from the oranges. Cut flesh into segments – do this over the mixing bowl to catch the juice.

7. Mix the orange segments with the fennel.

8. Add the olive oil and salt and mix together thoroughly.

9. Just before serving, divide the fennel-and-orange mixture evenly between the bread cases and garnish with fresh mint and fennel fronds.

TIME: Preparation takes 15 minutes, cooking takes 5 minutes.

VARIATIONS: Serve the salad on individual plates sprinkled with croutons.

COOK'S TIP: The salad can be made in advance and refrigerated until required, but do not fill the cases until just before serving.

SMOKED SALMON ROLLS WITH SHRIMP FILLING

This simply delicious appetizer will ensure guests feel spoiled without too much effort from the cook.

SERVES 4

1 cup frozen or fresh shelled, cooked shrimp
2 tbsps mayonnaise
1 tbsp whipped cream
2 tbsps tomato paste
Dash lemon juice
8 slices of smoked salmon, about 1 ounce each
Lemon wedges, sliced cucumber, and tomato for garnish.

1. Defrost the shrimp and drain if frozen.

2. Mix the mayonnaise, cream, tomato paste, and lemon juice in a bowl and fold in the shrimp.

3. Divide the mixture between the 8 slices of smoked salmon, placing it on top in a wedge shape, and rolling the salmon around it in a cone shape. Allow two for each person.

4. Garnish with lemon wedges, and sliced cucumber and tomato. Serve with thinly-sliced soda bread or ciabatta and butter.

TIME: Preparation takes 15 minutes.

SERVING IDEAS: Serve on its own as a appetizer, or with bread and salad for a light lunch or supper.

STUFFED EGGS

Stuffed eggs makes an attractive, and deliciously different, party appetizer.

MAKES 36

18 small eggs, or quail eggs
4 tbsps unsalted butter
1 clove garlic, crushed
⅓ cup cooked, peeled shrimp, finely
    chopped
½ tsp finely chopped fresh basil
Freshly ground black pepper, to taste

1. Cook the eggs in boiling water for 5 minutes. Drain, and plunge them immediately into cold water.

2. Allow the eggs to cool completely, then remove the shells. Rinse and drain.

3. Cut each egg in half lengthwise and carefully remove the yolks.

4. Put the yolks into a large bowl and beat in the butter and garlic. Mix well. This, and the next step, could be carried out in a food processor.

5. Add the shrimp, basil, and pepper to the creamed egg yolk mixture. Beat thoroughly until the consistency is soft.

6. Fill each egg-white half with a little of the prepared mixture, piling it attractively into the cavity left by the yolk.

7. Refrigerate until required.

TIME: Preparation takes 15 minutes, cooking takes 5 minutes.

VARIATIONS: Use flaked white crabmeat instead of the shrimp. For a more exotic dish, use quail eggs instead of hens' eggs.

SERVING IDEAS: Serve the filled egg halves on a plate which has been garnished with escarole, lollo rosso or oakleaf lettuce, and tiny pieces of sweet red pepper.

QUICK LIVER PÂTÉ

Liver sausage is lightly seasoned and smoked consistancy and is available with either a smooth or coarse consistancy.
It makes an "instant" pâté.

SERVES 4

11 ounces liver sausage
4 tbsps melted butter, preferably unsalted
2 tbsps brandy (optional)
1 clove garlic, crushed
Salt and pepper
Lettuce, cress or chia, and black olives for
　garnish

1. Place the sausage in a bowl with the butter, brandy, if using, garlic, salt, and pepper and beat until smooth. Alternatively, use a food processor.

2. Transfer the mixture to a piping bag fitted with a rosette nozzle.

3. Choose a large serving platter or individual plates and pipe out several swirls of pâté. Garnish with sliced or whole black olives, lettuce, and cress.

TIME: Preparation takes about 15 minutes.

COOK'S TIP: Always squeeze out the mixture from the top of the piping bag down to the nozzle. If the bag is held in the middle, the mixture will soften and melt, or it will burst out of the top.

SERVING IDEAS: Serve with hot toast fingers or thin slices of buttered rye bread. Instead of piping the pâté, serve it in individual ramekins.

MUSHROOMS IN SOUR CREAM

This very old recipe originally called for freshly-gathered forest mushrooms.

SERVES 4-6

6 cups button mushrooms, quartered

2 tbsps butter or margarine

6 green onions, thinly sliced

1 tbsp all-purpose flour

1 tbsp lemon juice

2 tbsps chopped fresh dill or 1 tbsp dried
   dill

Pinch salt and pepper

⅓ cup sour cream

4-6 slices buttered toast (optional)

Paprika

1. Rinse the mushrooms and pat dry well. Trim the stalks level with the caps before quartering. Melt the butter in a skillet and add the mushrooms and onions. Sauté for about 1 minute and stir in the flour.

2. Add the lemon juice, and all the remaining ingredients, except the sour cream and paprika. Cook slowly for about 1 minute.

3. Stir in the sour cream and adjust the seasoning. Heat through for about 1 minute. Spoon into individual serving dishes or pile on top of buttered toast. Sprinkle with paprika and serve immediately.

TIME: Preparation takes about 20 minutes, cooking takes about 5-7 minutes.

WATCHPOINT: Sour cream will curdle if boiled, although the addition of flour to the sauce will help to stabilize it somewhat.

SERVING IDEAS: Use as a side-dish or an appetizer with meat, poultry, or game. Prepare double quantity and serve with a salad and bread as a light lunch.

MUSSELS IN GINGER-CUMIN SAUCE

This delicious combination of seafood, wine, and spices makes for a mouthwatering start to a meal.

SERVES 4

6 cups mussels in their shells, scraped
2 shallots, chopped
1 bayleaf
⅓ cup dry white wine
2 tbsps butter
1 small piece ginger, grated
½tsp cumin
¼ tsp turmeric
½ green chili, seeded and chopped
Juice of ½ lime
⅔ cup heavy cream
Salt and pepper
2 tbsps minced parsley

1. Discard any mussels that are open or have cracked shells.

2. Put mussels into a large, deep pan and sprinkle with half the shallot. Add the bayleaf and wine.

3. Cover with a lid and bring to the boil, shaking the pan occasionally. Cook for about 3 minutes or until the mussels have opened. Set aside and keep covered.

4. Melt the butter in a saucepan and add the remaining chopped shallot. Soften for 2 minutes and add the ginger, cumin, turmeric, and chili.

5. Add the lime juice and the strained cooking liquid from the mussels. Bring to the boil, stirring occasionally, and allow to reduce by half.

6. Pour the cream over the mussels and reboil to reduce slightly and thicken.

7. Divide the mussels between 4 serving bowls and coat with the sauce.

8. Sprinkle parsley over each serving.

TIME: Preparation takes 20 minutes and cooking takes about 15 minutes.

SERVING IDEAS: Serve with whole-wheat French bread.

COOK'S TIP: Double the ingredients to serve 4 as an entrée.

MELON AND PROSCIUTTO

This is one of the best-loved Italian appetizers. It deserves to be, because the flavor of a ripe melon and the richness of Italian ham complement one another perfectly.

SERVES 4

1 large ripe melon
16 thin slices prosciutto ham

1. Cut the melon in half lengthwise, scoop out the seeds, and discard them.

2. Cut the melon into quarters and carefully pare away the rind. Cut each quarter into four slices.

3. Wrap each slice of melon in a slice of prosciutto and place on a serving platter. Alternatively, place the melon slices on the dish and cover with the slices of prosciutto, leaving the ends of the melon showing. Serve immediately.

TIME: Preparation takes about 20 minutes.

VARIATIONS: Place the slices of prosciutto flat on serving plates or roll them up into cigar shapes. Serve with quartered fresh figs instead of melon.

COOK'S TIP: Only use really ripe melon for this recipe, or the flavor will be insipid.

SPINACH GNOCCHI

Gnocchi are dumplings that are served like pasta. A dish of gnocchi can be served as a first course or as a light entrée, sprinkled with cheese or accompanied by a sauce.

SERVES 4-6

1 cup chopped, frozen spinach, defrosted
1 cup ricotta cheese
⅓ cup Parmesan cheese
Salt and pepper
Freshly-grated nutmeg
1 egg, lightly beaten
3 tbsps butter

1. Press the spinach between two plates to extract all the moisture.

2. Mix the spinach with the ricotta cheese, half the Parmesan cheese, salt, pepper, and nutmeg. Gradually add the egg, beating well until the mixture holds together when shaped.

3. With floured hands, shape the mixture into ovals, using about 1 tbsp mixture for each dumpling.

4. Lower into simmering water, 3 or 4 at a time, and allow to cook gently until the gnocchi float to the surface, about 1-2 minutes.

5. Remove with a perforated spoon and place in a well-buttered ovenproof dish.

6. When all the gnocchi are cooked, sprinkle them with the remaining Parmesan cheese and dot with the remaining butter.

7. Reheat for 10 minutes in a preheated 400°F oven, and brown under a pre-heated broiler before serving.

TIME: Preparation takes about 15 minutes, cooking takes about 20 minutes.

SERVING IDEAS: Accompany with a tomato or cheese sauce for a light meal with salad and hot bread.

COOK'S TIP: Gnocchi are best served soon after they are cooked. If allowed to stand overnight they become very heavy.

PASTA SHELLS WITH SEAFOOD

This speedy meal is excellent for informal entertaining.

SERVES 4

4 tbsps butter or margarine
2 cloves garlic, crushed
5 tbsps dry white wine
1¼ cups pouring cream
1 tbsp cornstarch
2 tbsps water
1 tbsp lemon juice
Salt and pepper
10 ounces pasta shells (conchiglie)
4 cups shrimp, shelled and de-veined
1 cup scallops, cleaned and sliced
1 tbsp minced parsley

1. Melt the butter in a pan. Add the garlic, and cook for 1 minute. Add the wine and cream, bring back to the boil, and cook for 2 minutes.

2. Mix the cornstarch with the water, and pour into the sauce. Stir until boiling. Add the lemon juice and salt and pepper to taste.

3. Meanwhile, cook the pasta in plenty of boiling, salted water, for about 10 minutes, or until tender. Drain, shaking to remove excess water.

4. Add the shrimp and scallops to the sauce and cook for 3 minutes.

5. Pour the sauce over the pasta shells, toss, and garnish with parsley before serving.

TIME: Preparation takes 5 minutes, cooking takes 15 minutes.

BUYING GUIDE: When buying fresh cooked shrimp ensure they are firm and brightly colored.

TURKEY MARSALA

Marsala is a dessert wine from Sicily which also complements turkey, veal, or chicken surprisingly well. It is traditional, but sherry will serve as a substitute if Marsala is unavailable.

SERVES 4

4 turkey scallops or breast fillets
4 tbsps butter or margarine
1 clove garlic
4 anchovy fillets, soaked in milk
4 slices Mozzarella cheese
Capers
2 tsps chopped marjoram
1 tbsp minced parsley
3 tbsps Marsala
⅔ cup heavy cream
Salt and pepper

1. If using the turkey breasts, flatten between two sheets of parchment or wax paper with a steak hammer or rolling pin.

2. Melt butter in a skillet and, when foaming, add the garlic and the turkey. Cook for a few minutes on each side until lightly browned. Remove them from the skillet.

3. Drain the anchovy fillets and rinse them well. Dry on kitchen paper. Place a slice of cheese on top of each turkey fillet and arrange the anchovies and capers on top of each. Sprinkle with the chopped herbs and return the turkey to the skillet.

4. Cook the turkey a further 5 minutes over moderate heat or until the turkey is cooked through, and the cheese has melted. Remove to a serving dish and keep warm.

5. Return the pan to the heat and add the Marsala to deglaze, then reduce the heat. Add the cream and whisk in well. Reduce the heat and simmer gently, uncovered, for a few minutes to thicken the sauce. Season the sauce with salt and pepper, and spoon it over the turkey fillets to serve.

TIME: Preparation takes about 25 minutes and cooking about 15 minutes.

WATCHPOINT: Turkey breast fillets are very lean so can dry out easily if overcooked.

SERVING IDEAS: Accompany the Turkey Marsala with new potatoes and lightly-cooked zucchini.

TROUT WITH CHIVE SAUCE

Chive sauce really complements trout and turns a simple dish into a speedy meal fit for a special occasion.

SERVES 4

4 even-sized rainbow trout, cleaned and
   fins trimmed
Flour mixed with salt and pepper for
   dredging
3 tbsps butter, melted
2 tbsps white wine
1¼ cups heavy cream
1 small bunch chives, snipped
Salt and pepper

1. Dredge the trout with the seasoned flour and place on a lightly-greased baking sheet. Spoon the melted butter over the fish.

2. Bake in a 400°F oven for about 10 minutes, basting frequently with the butter.

Cook until the skin is crisp. Check the fish on the underside close to the bone. If it is not cooked through, lower the oven temperature to 325°F for a further 5 minutes.

3. Pour the wine into a small saucepan and bring to the boil. Boil to reduce by half. Add the cream and bring back to the boil. Allow to boil rapidly until the sauce thickens slightly. Stir in the snipped chives, reserving some to sprinkle on top, if wished.

4. When the fish are browned, remove to a serving dish and spoon some of the sauce over them. Sprinkle with the reserved chives and serve the rest of the sauce separately.

TIME: Preparation takes 15 minutes and cooking takes 15-20 minutes.

VARIATIONS: Use this sauce with other fish such as salmon steaks or catfish.

SERVING IDEAS: Serve with boiled new potatoes and broccoli.

COD CURRY

The fragrant spices used in this recipe are now readily available at most supermarkets.

SERVES 4

1 large onion, chopped
3 tbsps vegetable oil
1-inch piece cinnamon stick
1 bayleaf
1 tsp ginger paste
1 tsp garlic paste
1 tsp chili powder
1 tsp ground cumin
1 tsp ground coriander
¼ tsp ground turmeric
⅔ cup plain yogurt
    or 1 cup canned tomatoes, chopped
1-2 fresh green chilies, chopped
2 sprigs fresh coriander leaves, chopped
1 pound cod cutlets, or fillets, cut into
    2-inch pieces
1 tsp salt

1. In a large heavy-based saucepan, sauté the onion in the oil until golden-brown. Add the cinnamon, bayleaf, and the ginger and garlic pastes, and cook for 1 minute.

2. Add the ground spices and cook for a further minute, then stir in *either* the yogurt, *or* the canned tomatoes, the chopped chilies, and coriander leaves.

3. Only if you have used yogurt, stir in ⅔ cup water and simmer the mixture for 2-3 minutes. Do not add any water if you have used the canned tomatoes.

4. Stir the cod into the sauce, and add the salt. Cover the pan and simmer for 15-18 minutes before serving.

TIME: Preparation takes about 15 minutes, and cooking takes about 20 minutes.

COOK'S TIP: Great care should be taken when preparing fresh chilies. Always wash hands thoroughly afterwards, and avoid getting any juice in the eyes or mouth. Rinse with copious amounts of clear water if this happens. For a milder curry, remove the seeds from the chili.

SERVING IDEAS: Serve with boiled rice and a cucumber salad.

BARBECUED SHRIMP

It's the sauce rather than the cooking method that gives the dish its name.
It's spicy, zippy and hot.

SERVES 2

4 cups jumbo shrimp, cooked and
  unpeeled
½ cup unsalted butter
1 tsp each white, black, and cayenne
  pepper
Pinch salt
1 tsp each chopped fresh thyme, rosemary,
  and marjoram
1 clove garlic, crushed
1 tsp Worcestershire sauce
⅔ cup fish broth
4 tbsps dry white wine
Cooked rice, to serve

1. Remove the eyes and the legs from the shrimp.

2. Melt the butter in a large skillet and add the white pepper, black pepper, cayenne pepper, salt, herbs, and garlic. Add the shrimp and toss over heat for a few minutes until heated through. Remove the shrimp and set them aside and keep warm.

3. Add the Worcestershire sauce, broth, and wine to the ingredients in the pan. Bring to the boil and cook for about 3 minutes to reduce. Add salt to taste.

4. Arrange the shrimp on a bed of rice and pour the sauce over them to serve.

TIME: Preparation takes about 15 minutes and cooking takes about 5 minutes.

PREPARATION: Because the shrimp are precooked, cook them very briefly again, just to heat through. Use uncooked, unpeeled shrimp if possible. Cook these until they curl and turn pink.

SERVING IDEAS: The shrimp may also be served cold, in which case prepare the sauce with 6 tbsps oil instead of butter.

LIVER VENEZIANA

*As the name indicates, this recipe originated in Venice. The lemon juice offsets
the rich taste of liver in this very famous Italian dish.*

SERVES 4-6

Risotto

3 tbsps butter or margarine

1 large onion, chopped

1 cup California or Carolina (risotto) rice

4 tbsps dry white wine

2⅔ cups chicken broth

¼ tsp saffron

Salt and pepper

2 tbsps grated fresh Parmesan cheese

Liver

1 pound calves' or lambs' liver

All-purpose flour for dredging

2 tbsps butter or margarine

2 tbsps oil

3 onions, thinly sliced

Juice of ½ a lemon

Salt and pepper

1 tbsp minced parsley

1. Melt the butter for the risotto in a large skillet, add the onion, and cook until soft but not colored, over gentle heat.

2. Add the rice and cook for about a minute until the rice looks transparent.

3. Add the wine, broth, saffron, and seasoning. Stir well and bring to the boil. Lower the heat and cook gently for about 20 minutes, stirring frequently, until the liquid has been absorbed.

4. Meanwhile, heat the butter or margarine and 1 tbsp oil in a large skillet, and cook the onions until golden.

5. Trim the liver and cut into very thin strips. Toss in a sieve with the flour to coat.

6. Remove the onions from the skillet to a platter. Add more oil if necessary, increase the heat under the pan, and add the liver. Cook, stirring constantly, for about 2 minutes.

7. Return the onions to the skillet, and add the lemon juice and parsley. Cook a further 2 minutes or until the liver is tender. Season with salt and pepper and serve with the risotto.

8. To finish the risotto, add the cheese and salt and pepper to taste when the liquid has been absorbed, and toss to melt the cheese.

TIME: Risotto takes about 30 minutes to prepare and cook. Liver takes about 4 minutes to cook.

WATCHPOINT: Liver needs only brief cooking or it will toughen.

PREPARATION: Tossing the liver and flour together in a sieve coats each piece of meat more evenly than can be done by hand.

COOK'S TIP: If wished add 4 tbsps stock to the recipe for a little more sauce.

SMOKED SALMON ROMA

*This quick dish has a fresh, light-tasting sauce, perfect for summer eating.
A simple green salad goes well with it.*

SERVES 4

1 small onion, minced
A little butter and oil for sautéing
2 zucchini, cut into sticks
Small bunch fresh dill, chopped
1 cup pouring cream mixed with 2 tbsps
    sour cream
Salt and black pepper
8 ounces smoked salmon, cut into strips
8 ounces fine ribbon pasta (linguine)
Lemon and dill to garnish

1. Sauté the onion in a little butter and oil until soft.

2. Add the zucchini and sauté for a few minutes. Do not overcook, they should remain crisp.

3. Add the chopped dill and the cream mixture, and gently heat through.

4. Season to taste and fold in the salmon strips. Keep warm.

5. Cook the pasta as directed on packet; drain.

6. Put the pasta in an oval dish and pour the sauce into the center. Decorate with lemon wedges and dill.

TIME: Preparation and cooking takes about 25 minutes.

VARIATIONS: Use different shapes of pasta such as bows, or whatever you
have to hand.

OVEN-BAKED SPAGHETTI

A convenient way to cook this favorite mid-week dish.

SERVES 4

8 ounces cooked whole-wheat spaghetti
2 × 14-ounce cans tomatoes, roughly
    chopped
1 large onion, grated
1 tsp oregano
Seasoning
½ cup Cheddar cheese
2 tbsps grated Parmesan cheese

1. Grease four individual ovenproof dishes and place a quarter of the spaghetti in each one.

2. Pour the tomatoes over the top.

3. Add the onion, sprinkle with oregano, and season well.

4. Slice the cheese finely and arrange over the top of the spaghetti mixture.

5. Sprinkle with Parmesan and bake at 350°F for 20-25 minutes.

TIME: Preparation takes 10 minutes, cooking takes 20-25 minutes.

SERVING IDEAS: Serve with garlic bread.

WATCHPOINT: When cooking spaghetti, remember to add a few drops of oil to the boiling water to stop it sticking together.

COOK'S TIP: Oven-baked Spaghetti may be cooked in one large casserole if required, in which case, add 10 minutes to the cooking time.

Shrimp and Ginger

Quick and easy to prepare, this dish is really delicious and also very nutritious.

SERVES 6

2 tbsps oil
6 cups peeled shrimp
1-inch piece fresh root ginger, peeled and
    finely chopped
2 garlic cloves, peeled and finely chopped
2-3 green onions, chopped
1 leek, white part only, cut into strips
½ cup garden peas
¾ cup bean sprouts
2 tbsps dark soy sauce
1 tsp sugar
Pinch salt

1. Heat the oil in a wok and stir-fry the shrimp for 2-3 minutes. Reserve the shrimp.

2. Reheat the oil and add the ginger and garlic. Stir quickly, then add the onions, leek, and peas. Stir-fry for 2-3 minutes.

3. Add the bean sprouts and shrimps to the cooked vegetables. Stir in the soy sauce, sugar, and salt, and cook for 2 minutes. Serve immediately.

TIME: Preparation takes about 10 minutes, and cooking takes about 7-9 minutes.

PREPARATION: The vegetables can be prepared in advance and kept in airtight plastic boxes in the refrigerator for up to 6 hours before needed.

SERVING IDEAS: Serve this on its own with rice or pasta, or as part of an authentic Chinese meal.

SPAGHETTI MARINARA

A delightful mix of seafood makes this dish special enough for any occasion, and it's quick and easy too!

SERVES 4

1½-ounce can anchovy fillets
5 tbsps water
5 tbsps dry white wine
1 bayleaf
4 peppercorns
8 ounces scallops, cleaned and sliced
2 tbsps olive oil
2 cloves garlic, crushed
1 tsp basil
1 x 14-ounce can plum tomatoes, de-seeded and chopped
1 tbsp tomato paste
10 ounces spaghetti
4 cups cooked shrimp, shelled and de-veined
1 tbsp minced parsley
Salt and pepper

1. Drain the anchovies and cut into small pieces.

2. Place water, wine, bayleaf, and peppercorns in a pan. Heat to a slow boil. Add the scallops and cook for 2 minutes. Remove and drain.

3. Heat the oil, add garlic and basil, and cook for 30 seconds. Add tomatoes, anchovies and tomato paste. Stir until combined. Cook for 10 minutes.

4. Meanwhile, cook the spaghetti in a large pan of boiling, salted water for 10 minutes, or until tender but still firm. Drain.

5. Add the seafood to sauce, and cook a further 1 minute, to heat through. Add parsley and stir through. Season with salt and pepper to taste. Toss gently.

6. Pour the sauce over the spaghetti and serve immediately, sprinkled with parsley.

TIME: Preparation takes 10 minutes, cooking takes 20 minutes.

VARIATIONS: Substitute the shrimp and scallops for the fresh mixed seafood now available in many supermarkets.

HAM AND GREEN BELL PEPPER OMELET

Served with salad and crusty French bread, this makes a tasty breakfast or lunch dish.

MAKES 1

3 eggs

2 tbsps milk

Freshly ground black pepper

1 tbsp vegetable oil

2 tbsps chopped green bell pepper

2 tomatoes, skinned, seeded, and coarsely
    chopped

2 tbsps diced lean ham

1. Break the eggs into a bowl and beat in the milk and pepper.

2. Heat the oil in an omelet pan and cook the green bell pepper until it is just soft.

3. Stir in the tomatoes and the ham. Heat through for 1 minute.

4. Pour the egg mixture into the omelet pan over the vegetables. Stir the mixture briskly with a wooden spoon, until it begins to cook.

5. As the egg begins to set, lift it slightly and tilt the pan to allow the uncooked egg to flow underneath.

6. When the egg on top is still slightly creamy, fold the omelet in half and slip it onto a serving plate. Serve immediately.

TIME: Preparation takes about 15 minutes, cooking takes 5 minutes.

COOK'S TIP: To peel tomatoes easily, cut a small cross in the skin and drop them into boiling water for about 10 seconds, then plunge into cold water. This loosens the skin.

VARIATIONS: Use any selection of your favorite vegetables to vary this delicious dish.

RICH PAN-FRIED STEAKS

Thin steaks are quickly fried and then cooked in a savory brown gravy.

SERVES 4

4-8 pieces frying steak, depending on size
1 tbsp oil
1 tbsp butter or margarine
1 tbsp all-purpose flour
6 green onions
1 clove garlic, crushed
1 tsp minced thyme
2 tsps minced parsley
3 tomatoes, skinned, seeded, and chopped
1¼ cups beef broth
Dash of Tabasco
Salt and pepper

1. Place the meat between 2 sheets of parchment or wax paper and pound with a rolling pin or a steak hammer to flatten slightly.

2. Heat the oil in a large skillet and brown the meat quickly, a few pieces at a time. Set the meat aside.

3. Melt the butter or margarine in the skillet and add the flour. Cut the white part off the green onions and chop it finely. Add to the flour and butter, reserving the green onion tops for later use.

4. Add the garlic to the skillet and cook the mixture slowly, stirring frequently until it is a dark golden-brown. Add the herbs, tomatoes, broth, Tabasco, and salt and pepper to taste, and bring to the boil. Cook for about 5 minutes to thicken, and then add the steaks. Cook to heat the meat through.

5. Chop the green tops of the green onions and sprinkle over the steaks to garnish.

TIME: Preparation takes about 20 minutes and cooking takes about 20 minutes.

SERVING IDEAS: Serve with rice or potatoes. Add a green vegetable or salad.

VARIATIONS: Add chopped red or green bell pepper to the sauce.

Sautéed Lemon Pork

A perfect way to prepare this tender cut of pork. You may be able to find a butcher to beat the meat for you, or do it yourself with a steak hammer.

SERVES 4

8 small pork tenderloin or steaks, beaten
    until thin
Flour for dredging
Salt and pepper
2 tbsps butter or margarine
1 green bell pepper, thinly sliced
6 tbsps dry white wine or sherry
1 tbsp lemon juice
¾ cup chicken broth
1 lemon, peeled and thinly sliced

1. Dredge the pork with a mixture of flour, salt, and pepper. Shake off the excess.

2. Melt the butter or margarine in a large skillet and brown the pork, a few pieces at a time. Remove the meat and keep it warm.

3. Cook the green pepper slices briefly and set aside with the pork.

4. Pour the wine or sherry and lemon juice into the skillet to deglaze. Add the broth and bring to the boil. Boil for 5 minutes to reduce. Add the pork and peppers and cook for 15 minutes over gentle heat. Add the lemon slices and heat through before serving.

TIME: Preparation takes about 25 minutes and cooking takes about 20-25 minutes.

PREPARATION: Cut off all the rind and white parts of the lemon, using a sharp knife, before slicing the flesh.

VARIATIONS: Use red pepper instead of green pepper and add chopped green onions.

MACARONI CHEESE WITH ANCHOVIES

Anchovies add extra flavor to this much-loved dish.

SERVES 4

2 ounces canned anchovy fillets
8 ounces macaroni
¼ cup butter or margarine
4 tbsps all-purpose flour
2½ cups milk
½ tsp dry mustard
¾ cup yellow cheese, shredded
Salt and pepper

1. Drain the anchovies, and set enough aside to slice in half and make a thin lattice over the dish. Chop the rest finely.

2. Cook the macaroni in plenty of boiling, salted water for 10 minutes, or until tender but still firm. Rinse in hot water and drain well.

3. Meanwhile, melt the butter in a pan. Stir in the flour and cook for 1 minute.

4. Remove from the heat, and gradually stir in the milk. Return to the heat and bring to the boil. Simmer for 3 minutes, stirring occasionally.

5. Stir in the mustard, anchovies, and half the cheese. Season with salt and pepper to taste. Stir in the macaroni, and pour into an ovenproof dish.

6. Sprinkle the remaining cheese over the top, and make a latticework with the remaining anchovies. Brown under a hot broiler. Serve immediately.

TIME: Preparation takes 5 minutes, cooking takes 15 minutes.

SERVING IDEAS: Serve this hearty dish with crusty bread and a mixed green salad.

CHICKEN WITH CHERRIES

Canned cherries make an easy sauce that makes chicken really fancy.

SERVES 6

Oil
6 chicken breasts, skinned and boned
1 sprig fresh rosemary
Grated rind and juice of ½ a lemon
⅔ cup red wine
Salt and pepper
4 cups canned black cherries, pitted
2 tsps cornstarch

1. Heat about 4 tbsps oil in a skillet over moderate heat. Add the chicken breasts, skin side down first. Cook until just lightly browned. Turn over and cook the second side about 2 minutes.

2. Remove any oil remaining in the pan and add the rosemary, lemon rind, wine, and salt and pepper. Bring to the boil and then reduce the heat.

3. Add the cherries and their juice. Cover and cook for 15 minutes or until the chicken is tender. Remove the chicken and cherries and keep them warm. Discard the rosemary.

4. Mix the cornstarch and lemon juice. Add several spoonfuls of the hot sauce to the cornstarch mixture. Return the mixture to the skillet and bring to the boil, stirring constantly, until thickened and cleared.

5. Pour the sauce over the chicken and cherries. Heat through and serve.

TIME: Preparation takes about 10 minutes and cooking takes about 20 minutes.

PREPARATION: Serve the chicken dish on the day that it is cooked – it does not keep well.

SERVING IDEAS: Serve with plain boiled rice. Accompany with a green vegetable, such as lightly steamed snow peas.

VEAL SCALOPPINE WITH PROSCIUTTO AND CHEESE

Veal is the meat used most often in Italian cooking. Good veal is tender and cooks quickly but it is expensive. Save this recipe for your next dinner party!

SERVES 4

8 veal scallops
2 tbsps butter or margarine
1 clove garlic, crushed
8 slices prosciutto ham
3 tbsps sherry
⅔ cup beef broth
1 sprig rosemary
8 slices Mozzarella cheese
Salt and pepper

1. Pound the veal escalopes out thinly between two pieces of parchment or wax paper with a steak hammer or a rolling pin.

2. Melt the butter or margarine in a skillet and add the veal and garlic. Cook until the veal is lightly browned on both sides.

3. Place a piece of prosciutto on top of each piece of veal and add the sherry, broth, and sprig of rosemary to the pan. Cover the pan and cook the veal for about 10 minutes over gentle heat or until tender and cooked through.

4. Remove the meat to a warmed heatproof serving platter and top each piece of veal with a slice of cheese.

5. Bring the cooking liquid from the veal to the boil, season and allow to boil rapidly to reduce slightly.

6. Meanwhile, grill the veal to melt and brown the cheese. Remove the sprig of rosemary from the sauce and pour the sauce around the meat to serve.

TIME: Preparation takes about 15 minutes, cooking takes 15-20 minutes.

VARIATIONS: White wine may be substituted for the sherry, if wished, and 1 tsp of tomato purée may be added to the sauce. Use chicken, turkey or pork instead of the veal.

CRUNCHY COD

Cod provides the perfect base for a crunchy, slightly spicy topping.

SERVES 4

4 even-sized cod fillets
Salt and pepper
⅓ cup melted butter
⅔ cup dry breadcrumbs
1 tsp dry mustard
1 tsp minced onion
Dash each Worcestershire sauce and
   Tabasco
2 tbsps lemon juice
1 tbsp minced parsley

1. Season the fish fillets with salt and pepper and place them on a grill pan. Brush with some of the butter and grill for about 5 minutes.

2. Combine the remaining butter with the breadcrumbs, mustard, onion, Worcestershire sauce, Tabasco, lemon juice and parsley.

3. Spoon the mixture carefully on top of each fish fillet, covering it completely. Press down lightly to pack the crumbs into place. Grill for a further 5-7 minutes, or until the top is lightly browned and the fish flakes.

TIME: Preparation takes about 15 minutes and cooking takes about 12 minutes.

PREPARATION: If wished, the fish may also be baked in the oven at 350°F. Cover the fish with foil for the first 5 minutes of baking time, then uncover and top with the breadcrumb mixture. Bake for a further 10-12 minutes.

VARIATIONS: The breadcrumb topping may be used on other fish such as red snapper, sea bream, or grouper.

BROCCOLI AND CAULIFLOWER SALAD

Serve this simple salad with graham crackers.

SERVES 4

1 red bell pepper
3 cups broccoli
3 cups cauliflower
1 tbsp roasted almond flakes

Dressing
4 tbsps thickset plain yogurt
2 tbsps lemon juice
2 tbsps olive oil
Salt and pepper
Pinch of nutmeg

1. Cut the pepper into matchstick pieces.

2. Wash and trim the broccoli and cauliflower and break into small flowerets.

3. Place the pepper, broccoli, and cauliflower in a mixing bowl.

4. Combine the yogurt, lemon juice, olive oil, seasoning, and nutmeg in a screwtop jar and shake well or combine in a blender.

5. Spoon the dressing over the salad and mix together well.

6. Divide the mixture between 4 individual serving dishes and garnish with the almond flakes.

TIME: Preparation takes 10 minutes.

VARIATIONS: Omit the nutmeg from the dressing and add a few freshly chopped herbs.

COOK'S TIP: If preparing this salad in advance, don't garnish with the almonds until serving time.

KENSINGTON SALAD

This salad has plenty of crunch to it and a lovely tangy dressing.

SERVES 2-3

3 large mushrooms, thinly sliced
1 medium eating apple, cut into chunks and
    dipped in lemon juice
2 celery sticks, cut into matchsticks
2 tbsps walnut pieces
1 bunch watercress

Dressing

1 tbsp mayonnaise
1 tbsp thickset plain yogurt
½ tsp Dijon-style mustard
A little lemon juice
Salt and pepper

1. Place the mushrooms, apple, celery, and walnuts in a bowl.

2. Combine all the ingredients for the dressing, and toss lightly with the vegetables.

3. Arrange the watercress on a flat serving platter and pile the salad mixture on the top.

TIME: Preparation takes about 10 minutes.

VARIATIONS: A medium bulb of fennel, thinly sliced, could be used in place of the celery.

SERVING IDEAS: Decorate the top of this salad with sliced strawberries or kiwi fruits.

GREEK COUNTRY SALAD

Lettuce is shredded finely for salads in Greece. In fact, the finer the shreds of lettuce, the better the salad is considered to be.

SERVES 4

2 tbsps olive oil
1 tbsp lemon juice
Salt and ground black pepper
1 clove garlic, crushed
1 romaine lettuce, well washed
3 tomatoes, sliced
⅓ cup black olives
½ cup feta cheese, diced
½ red bell pepper, sliced
6 peperonata
Fresh or dried oregano

1. Whisk the oil, lemon juice, salt and pepper, and garlic together until well emulsified. A blender or food processor may be used.

2. Stack up 5 or 6 lettuce leaves and shred them finely with a sharp knife.

3. Place the lettuce in the bottom of a serving dish and arrange the other ingredients on top. Pour the dressing over the mixture and sprinkle on the oregano.

TIME: Preparation takes about 10-15 minutes.

BUYING GUIDE: Peperonata are small whole peppers preserved in brine. They can be bought bottled in delicatessens and some supermarkets.

VARIATIONS: Substitute green bell pepper for red bell pepper if wished. Other varieties of lettuce may also be used.

GREEN-AND-GOLD SUNFLOWER SALAD

*This colorful salad makes a spectacular and delicious addition
to a summer meal.*

SERVES 4

3 tbsps sunflower oil
1 tbsp lemon juice
Salt and pepper
2 large ripe avocados
8 ripe apricots
⅓ cup plain yogurt
2 tsps honey
Grated rind of 1 lemon
2 tsps minced parsley
1 small Boston lettuce, washed and
    separated into leaves
4 tbsps roasted sunflower seeds

1. Put the oil and lemon juice into a small bowl with the salt and pepper. Mix together well.

2. Cut the avocados in half and pit them. Peel them, cut into slices, and mix these into the oil-and-lemon-juice dressing very carefully, taking care not to break them.

3. Cut the apricots in half and pit them. If the apricots are large, cut them in half again. Add them to the avocados in the dressing.

4. In another bowl, mix together the yogurt, honey, lemon rind, and parsley.

5. Put the lettuce leaves onto individual salad plates and arrange the avocado and apricots on top in a sunflower design.

6. Spoon a little of the yogurt mixture over the salad, and sprinkle with sunflower seeds. Pour any remaining yogurt dressing into a small pitcher, and serve separately.

TIME: Preparation takes about 15 minutes.

VARIATIONS: Use segments of ruby grapefruit in place of the apricots.

SERVING IDEAS: Serve as an unusual first course, or as an accompaniment to a chicken or fish dish.

RICE AND NUT SALAD

This refreshing salad is high in protein from the rice, nuts, and beans, so it could be eaten as a vegetarian main course.

SERVES 4

2 tbsps olive oil

2 tbsps lemon juice

Freshly ground sea salt and black pepper

½ cup yellow raisins

2 tbsps currants

1½ cups cooked brown rice, well drained

⅓ cup blanched almonds, chopped

2 tbsps cashew nuts, chopped

2 tbsps chopped walnuts

15-ounce can peach slices in natural juice, drained and chopped

¼ cucumber, cubed

½ cup cooked red kidney beans

A few pitted black olives

1. Put the olive oil, lemon juice, and salt and pepper into a screwtop jar. Shake vigorously, until the mixture has thickened or process in a blender.

2. Put the yellow raisins and the currants into a small bowl, and cover with boiling water. Allow to stand for 10 minutes, before draining the fruit.

3. Mix together the rice, nuts, soaked fruit, peaches, cucumber, kidney beans, and olives in a large mixing bowl.

4. Pour the dressing over the salad, and mix together thoroughly, to ensure all the ingredients are evenly coated.

TIME: Preparation will take about 15 minutes.

PREPARATION: For a more unusual flavor, soak the yellow raisins and currants in hot jasmine tea, instead of water.

VARIATIONS: Use a 15-ounce can of apricot halves in natural juice, in place of the can of peaches.

SERVING IDEAS: Serve the salad on a bed of crisp lettuce, or chopped chicory.

CREAMY SWEETCORN AND PEPPERS

*Sweetcorn is essential to this recipe, but other vegetables can be added, too.
Choose your favorites or use what you have to hand.*

SERVES 6

4 tbsps oil
2 tbsps butter
2 medium onions, minced
1 clove garlic, crushed
1 medium green pepper, cut into small dice
6 tomatoes, skinned, de-seeded, and diced
1 cup frozen corn kernels
1¼ cups chicken or vegetable broth
Pinch salt
4 tbsps heavy cream
Pinch of paprika

1. Heat the oil in a deep pot or Dutch oven and add the butter. When foaming, add the onions and garlic and cook, stirring frequently, for about 5 minutes or until both are soft and transparent but not browned.

2. Add the green pepper, tomatoes, corn, and broth. Bring to the boil over high heat.

3. Reduce the heat, partially cover the pot, and allow to cook slowly for about 10 minutes, or until the corn is tender. Add salt and stir in the cream. Heat through, sprinkle with paprika, and serve immediately.

TIME: Preparation takes about 25 minutes. Cooking takes about 10 minutes.

VARIATIONS: Use canned tomatoes, coarsely chopped.

COOK'S TIP: Sweetcorn toughens if cooked at too high a temperature for too long, or if boiled too rapidly.

STRAWBERRY CLOUD

It takes no time at all to make this delightful summer dessert.

SERVES 4-6

4 cups strawberries
1½ cups silken tofu
Juice of ½ lemon
2 tbsps soft brown sugar
Few drops vanilla extract

1. Wash and hull the strawberries. Reserve a few for the garnish.

2. Drain the tofu and blend it in a liquidizer together with the strawberries, lemon juice, and sugar.

3. Liquidize until smooth.

4. Add vanilla extract to taste and mix well.

5. Divide the mixture between 4-6 individual serving dishes and decorate with the reserved strawberries.

6. Chill until required.

TIME: Preparation takes 5-8 minutes.

SERVING IDEAS: For a special occasion, pipe whipped cream around the edges of the serving dishes.

VARIATIONS: Other fruits, such as apples or peaches, may be used instead but they will not produce such a colorful dessert.

COOK'S TIP: Substitute cream cheese for tofu if wished and add lemon juice to taste.

BROWN SUGAR BANANAS

Bananas in a rich brown sugar sauce make a delectable dessert.

SERVES 4

4 ripe bananas, peeled
Lemon juice
½ cup butter
½ packed cup soft brown sugar, light or
    dark
Pinch each ground cinnamon and nutmeg
⅔ cup orange juice
4 tbsps white or dark rum
Juice of ½ lemon
⅔ cup whipped cream
2 tbsps chopped pecans

1. Cut the bananas in half lengthwise and sprinkle all over with lemon juice.

2. Melt the butter in a large skillet and add the sugar, cinnamon, nutmeg, and orange juice. Stir over gentle heat until the sugar dissolves into a syrup.

3. Add the banana halves and cook gently for about 3 minutes, basting the bananas often with syrup, but not turning them.

4. Once the bananas are heated through, warm the rum in a small saucepan and ignite with a match. Pour the flaming rum over the bananas and shake the pan gently until the flames die down naturally. Place 2 banana halves on each serving plate and top with some of the whipped cream. Sprinkle with pecans and serve immediately.

TIME: Preparation takes about 15 minutes; cooking takes about 5 minutes for the sugar-and-butter syrup, and 3-4 minutes for the bananas.

SERVING IDEAS: The bananas may be served with vanilla ice cream instead of whipped cream, if wished.

COOK'S TIP: Sprinkling the cut surfaces of the banana with lemon juice keeps them from turning brown, and also offsets the sweetness of the sauce.

SWEET ALMOND DESSERT

A delicious variation on a traditional rice pudding, perfect for the cold winter months.

SERVES 4

¾ cup blanched almonds
2 cups water
¾ cup sugar
3 tbsps ground rice
⅔ cup milk

1. Blend the blanched almonds and the water in a liquidizer or food processor, until the almonds are well chopped.

2. Put the almond liquid into a medium-sized saucepan and bring this mixture to the boil over a gentle heat.

3. Add the sugar and stir until it has completely dissolved.

4. Combine the rice and the milk in a pitcher.

5. Add the rice mixture slowly to the simmering sugar and almond mixture, stirring continuously, until the pudding thickens.

6. Remove the almond pudding from the heat and pour into individual dessert dishes.

TIME: Preparation takes about 5 minutes, and cooking takes 6-7 minutes.

VARIATIONS: Lightly toast some flaked or chopped almonds and sprinkle these over the top of the dessert to serve.

SERVING IDEAS: Serve this dessert cold with fresh or stewed fruit.

CRÊPES

These tasty pancakes are delicious with both sweet and tangy sauces.

MAKES 10-12 PANCAKES

1 cup all-purpose flour
Pinch salt
1 egg
⅔ cup milk
1 tsp vegetable oil
Juice and zested rind of 1 lemon and 1
    orange

1. Sift the flour and the salt into a large bowl and make a well in the center.

2. Put the egg and the milk into a pitcher and beat well.

3. Gradually pour the egg and milk mixture into the center of the bowl and mix it in gently, stirring and drawing in the flour from the sides, until all has been incorporated. Beat to ensure even mixing.

4. Heat a little oil in a small skillet or omelet pan, and add enough mixture to make a thin pancake.

5. Quickly tilt and rotate the skillet so that the mixture coats the bottom of it evenly.

6. Cook the pancake over a moderate heat until the underside has turned brown and the top has set.

7. Carefully turn the pancake over and brown the other side in the same way.

8. Turn each pancake out onto parchment paper and keep them warm until required.

9. Serve the pancakes hot with freshly squeezed orange and lemon juice and decorate with the rinded citrus rind.

TIME: Preparation takes approximately 10 minutes, cooking takes about 20 minutes for all the pancakes.

WATCHPOINT: Do not overheat your skillet or the base of the pancake will burn before the top has set. Also, do not attempt to turn the pancake until the underside is properly cooked.

TO FREEZE: Make the pancakes in greater quantities than this recipe, and freeze, interleaved with wax or parchment paper, until required.

ALMOND-STUFFED FIGS

Fresh mission figs from California are in season in the fall. When ripe, they go a luscious purple black and are soft to the touch.

SERVES 4

4 large ripe mission figs
4 tbsps ground almonds
2 tbsps orange juice
2 tbsps finely chopped dried apricots
4 tbsps plain yogurt
Finely grated rind ½ orange
Wedges of figs, and mint or strawberry
    leaves for decoration

1. Cut each fig into quarters using a sharp knife, taking care not to cut right down through the base.

2. Ease the four sections of each fig outward to form a flower shape.

3. Put the ground almonds, orange juice, and chopped apricots into a small bowl and mix together thoroughly.

4. Divide this mixture into four, and press it into the center of each fig.

5. For the sauce, mix the yogurt with the orange rind, and thin it down with just a little water, or orange juice.

6. Spoon a small pool of orange yogurt onto each of four plates, and place a stuffed fig into the center of each pool. Decorate with the additional wedges of fig, and the mint or strawberry leaves.

TIME: Preparation takes approximately 20 minutes.

VARIATIONS: Use peach halves instead of the figs in this recipe.

WATCHPOINT: Do not add too much water or orange juice to the sauce, or it will become too thin.

OATLET COOKIES

A delicious mixture of oatmeal, seeds, and syrup makes these cookies extra special.

MAKES 10 COOKIES

1 cup raw oatmeal
1 cup all-purpose flour
6 tbsps sunflower seeds
1 tbsp sesame seeds
½ tsp mixed spice
½ cup margarine
1 tbsp brown sugar
1 tsp golden syrup or molasses
½ tsp baking powder
1 tbsp boiling water
2 cups chocolate drops or kisses

1. Mix the raw oatmeal, flour, sunflower seeds, sesame seeds, and spice together.

2. Melt the margarine, sugar, and golden syrup or molasses over a gentle heat.

3. Add the baking powder and water to the syrup mixture and stir well.

4. Pour this over dry ingredients and mix.

5. Place spoonfuls of the mixture, spaced well apart, on a greased cookie sheet and bake for 10 minutes at 375°F.

6. Allow to cool on the sheet.

7. Melt the chocolate drops or kisses in a bowl over hot water and place teaspoonsful of the melted chocolate on top of the cookies. Leave to set. Store in an airtight tin.

TIME: Preparation takes 15 minutes, cooking takes 10 minutes.

VARIATIONS: Ground ginger can be used in place of the mixed spice.

COOK'S TIP: Squares of cooking chocolate may be used in place of the chocolate drops or kisses.

SHORTBREADS

Sandwich these cookies together with raspberry jam for children's birthday parties.

MAKES ABOUT 18

1¼ cups all-purpose flour
½ cup light brown sugar
½ cup soft margarine
½ tsp vanilla extract

1. Sift the flour and sugar together and rub the margarine into the mixture.

2. Add the vanilla extract and bind the mixture together.

3. Form into small balls and place on a cookie sheet a few inches apart.

4. With the back of a fork, press the balls down making a criss-cross pattern.

5. Bake in a pre-heated oven at 375°F for about 10-15 minutes until golden-brown in color.

6. Cool on a wire rack.

TIME: Preparation takes 10 minutes, cooking takes 10-15 minutes.

VARIATIONS: Add 1 tablespoon of currants to make fruit cookies. Omit the vanilla extract and substitute almond extract to make almond shortbreads.

COOK'S TIP: Store these cookies in an airtight container.

YOGURT SCONES

These sweet biscuits make a delicious alternative to cookies.

MAKES 10 SCONES

4 tbsps butter
2 cups whole-wheat flour
1 tsp baking powder
1 tbsp brown sugar
2 tbsps raisins
Plain yogurt to mix

1. Rub the butter into the flour and sugar.

2. Add the raisins and mix well.

3. Slowly stir in enough yogurt to make to a fairly stiff dough.

4. Turn the mixture onto a floured board and knead lightly.

5. Roll out the dough to about ¾-inch thick and cut into 2-inch rounds.

6. Place on a lightly greased cookie sheet and bake near the top of the oven at 425°F for 14-16 minutes.

7. Remove from the cookie sheet and cool on a wire rack. Serve warm.

TIME: Preparation takes 10 minutes, cooking takes 14-16 minutes.

VARIATIONS: Use chopped dried apricots instead of raisins.

SERVING IDEAS: Serve with jam and cream.

Photography by Peter Barry
Recipes by Judith Ferguson, Patricia Payne and Fréderic Lebain
Designed by Richard Hawke
Edited by Jillian Stewart

PASTA

COOKING

® Landoll, Inc.
Ashland, Ohio 44805

Contents

Introduction

Pasta has become increasingly popular over the last few years. Pasta is literally a paste made with flour and eggs. Commercial pasta is usually made from hard durum wheat, but fresh pasta can be made with almost any kind of flour. It can also be made in a variety of different colors with the addition of ingredients such as spinach and tomato paste.

You can make pasta at home, but it is often more convenient to buy the fresh varieties now available in supermarkets. A wide range of dried, packaged pastas are also on offer, but these do not match the taste of the real thing! Pasta comes in a bewildering array of names and shapes. Because the Italian names often vary depending on which region the pasta originates from, it is often easier to look for the shape of the particular pasta you require.

Pasta is the perfect complement to a wide range of other ingredients. It can simply be mixed with olive oil and garlic or fresh herbs, or it can be enhanced with everything from tomatoes and cheese to ham and olives. Tomatoes, cheese and herbs are the most common ingredients in pasta sauces and fillings, but even within these categories there are numerous flavors and uses. Parmesan is treasured for its wonderful flavor, while ricotta is perfect for stuffing pasta as it adds body and holds its shape well. One of the joys of cooking pasta is that it combines so well with numerous ingredients, so experiment with your favorites to find flavors that you enjoy.

One of the bonuses of pasta is that it is simple and quick to cook, but a few guidelines should be followed. Never overcook pasta as it will quickly become sticky. Remember that fresh pasta cooks more quickly than the dried variety. Whole wheat pasta takes longer to cook and cooking times will also vary according to the thickness of the pasta. Most important, pasta should be cooked in a large, uncovered saucepan of boiling, salted water. A little olive oil can be added to prevent the pasta sticking, and the water boiling over.

The ease of cooking and variety of shapes and flavors ensures that pasta is here to stay, so start experimenting with some of the recipes in this book, and you will find that producing the perfect pasta dish is simplicity itself.

MEATBALL SOUP

*A filling soup which makes a meal
in itself when served with bread.*

SERVES 4

---

1 lb beef bones (see Cook's Tip)
1 carrot
1 onion, chopped
1 celery stalk, chopped
1 egg, beaten
½ lb ground beef
½ cup bread crumbs
Salt and pepper
1 tbsp oil
14 oz can crushed plum tomatoes
¾ cup small pasta
1 tbsp chopped fresh parsley

---

1. Place bones, carrot, onion and celery in a large saucepan and cover with cold water. Bring to a boil, cover and simmer for at least one hour.

2. Meanwhile, mix lightly beaten egg with ground beef, bread crumbs and plenty of seasoning.

3. Take a teaspoon of the mixture and roll into small balls. Heat oil in a roasting pan and put in the balls. Bake in a preheated oven at 350°F for 45 minutes, turning occasionally.

4. Strain stock into a saucepan.

5. Add tomatoes to stock. Bring to a boil, and simmer for 15 minutes. Add pasta and cook for 10 minutes, stirring frequently.

6. Add meatballs, adjust seasoning, and stir in chopped parsley. Serve hot.

TIME: Preparation takes 10 minutes, cooking takes 1 hour 40 minutes.

COOK'S TIP: Use a beef stock cube instead of the beef bones. Dissolve the stock cube in a little boiling water, add to the saucepan with the vegetables and cover with cold water.

MINESTRA

*Some of Italy's finest ingredients
make up this warming soup.*

SERVES 4

1 onion
1 carrot
1 celery stalk
2 tbsps olive oil
6 cups water
Salt and pepper
½ lb fresh spinach
2 tomatoes
4 oz elbow macaroni
2 cloves garlic, crushed
2 tbsps chopped fresh parsley
1 tsp fresh rosemary or ½ tsp dried
¼ cup Parmesan cheese, grated

1. Cut onion, carrot and celery into thick, julienne.

2. Heat oil in a large, heavy pan and fry vegetable strips until just brown, stirring occasionally. Pour on water, season with salt and pepper, and simmer for 20 minutes.

3. Meanwhile, wash and cut spinach leaves into shreds, add to soup and simmer for 10 minutes.

4. Blanch and peel tomatoes and chop coarsely, removing seeds.

5. Add tomatoes, macaroni, garlic, parsley and rosemary to the soup, and simmer another 10 minutes. Adjust seasoning. Serve with grated Parmesan cheese if desired.

TIME: Preparation takes 15 minutes, cooking takes 45 minutes.

MACARONI WITH OLIVE SAUCE

Macaroni is served here with butter, garlic and finely chopped olives.
A very tasty dish that makes an ideal appetizer.

SERVES 4

11 oz macaroni
¼ cup butter
1 clove garlic, finely chopped
10 pitted olives, green and/or black, finely
   chopped
Salt and pepper

1. Cook the macaroni to your liking in salted, boiling water. Rinse in hot water and set aside to drain.

2. Melt the butter in a saucepan and add the garlic and olives. Cook for 1 minute and then stir in the macaroni.

3. Check the seasoning, adding salt and pepper as necessary. Serve hot.

TIME: Preparation takes about 10 minutes, cooking takes approximately 20 minutes.

VARIATION: Add a few chopped capers to the olives, but reduce the amount of salt.

COOK'S TIP: Rinse the macaroni really well under hot water to prevent it from sticking together.

VERMICELLI PESCATORE

*This impressive dish is simple to prepare
and perfect for special guests.*

SERVES 4

12 mussels
12 clams
½ lb cod fillets
¼ lb squid, cleaned
4 large shrimp, cooked
4 fresh oysters, cooked
3 cups tomato sauce
¼ cup olive oil
1 cup dry white wine
Half a green pepper, diced
Salt and pepper
9 oz package vermicelli

1. Prepare seafood. If using fresh mussels, clean closed mussels, removing beard, and cook in boiling water for 3 minutes until they open. (Discard any that remain closed).

2. Cool and remove from shells, keeping a few in shells for garnish if desired. Cut cod into ½ inch pieces.

3. Cut squid into rings.

4. Heat 2 tbsps oil in a pan and add the squid. Fry gently until golden brown, then add wine, tomato sauce, green pepper, and salt and pepper to taste. Simmer for 20 minutes and then add cod. Simmer for another 10 minutes, stirring occasionally.

5. Add clams and mussels and bring mixture back to a boil; adjust seasoning. Meanwhile, cook vermicelli in plenty of boiling, salted water for 10 minutes, or until tender but still firm. Drain well. Add seafood mixture and toss. Garnish with shrimps and oysters.

TIME: Preparation takes 15 minutes, cooking takes 40 minutes.

CABBAGE AND PASTA SOUP

*Chicken stock flavored with bacon, cabbage, pasta and
garlic is the base for this light and tasty appetizer.*

SERVES 4

6 leaves white cabbage
1 tbsp olive oil
5 oz small pasta shells
2 slices bacon
1 clove garlic, chopped
3 cups chicken stock
Salt and pepper

1. Cut the cabbage into thin strips. To do
this, roll the leaves into cigar shapes and
cut with a very sharp knife.

2. Heat the olive oil. Trim excess fat from
bacon, dice meat and fry the bacon, garlic
and cabbage together for 2 minutes.

3. Pour over the stock, season with salt
and pepper and cook on a moderate heat
for 15 minutes.

4. Add the pasta to the soup and cook for
another 15 minutes.

5. Check the seasoning and serve.

TIME: Preparation takes about 5 minutes, cooking takes approximately 35 minutes.

SERVING IDEA: Sprinkle over a little grated Parmesan cheese just before serving the soup.

VARIATION: Leave the piece of bacon whole and remove before serving the soup.

CHICK PEA SOUP

This unusual sounding soup is a wonderful mixture
of chick peas and classic Italian ingredients.

SERVES 4

1 cup dried chick peas
3 tbsps olive oil
2 cloves garlic
1½ cups plum tomatoes, chopped
3 cups water
1 tsp fresh basil or ½ tsp dried
1 chicken bouillon cube
Salt and pepper
1 cup small pasta or elbow macaroni
2 tbsps Parmesan cheese, grated

1. Soak chick peas overnight in enough water to cover by 1 inch. Drain and discard water. Place the chick peas in a large, heavy pan, and cover with 1 inch of water. Bring to a boil and simmer, covered, for about 1 hour until chick peas are tender. Make sure they do not boil dry.

2. Heat olive oil in a heavy pan and sauté garlic cloves. When browned, remove and discard garlic cloves. Add tomatoes and their juice, water and basil, and simmer for 20 minutes.

3. Add drained chick peas, crumbled bouillon cube, and salt and pepper to taste. Stir well and simmer another 10 minutes. Bring back to a boil. Add pasta and cook, stirring frequently, for 10 minutes.

4. Mix in half of the Parmesan cheese. Adjust seasoning and serve immediately, with remaining Parmesan cheese sprinkled on top.

TIME: Preparation takes overnight soaking for the chick peas plus 5 minutes, cooking takes 1 hour 20 minutes.

COOK'S TIP: Soup may be puréed before pasta is added, if desired.

BEAN SOUP

*Kidney beans and pasta combine to produce
a filling soup suitable for all the family.*

SERVES 4-6

15 oz can kidney beans
2 slices bacon, chopped
1 celery stalk, chopped
1 small onion, chopped
1 clove garlic, crushed
½ cup plum tomatoes, chopped
   and seeds removed
1 tbsp chopped fresh parsley
1 tsp fresh basil or ½ tsp dried
4 cups water
1 chicken bouillon cube
Salt and pepper
1 cup whole wheat pasta

1. Place kidney beans, bacon, celery, onion, garlic, parsley, basil, tomatoes and water in a large saucepan. Bring to a boil and add bouillon cube and salt and pepper to taste. Cover and cook on a low heat for about 1½ hours.

2. Raise heat and add pasta, stirring well. Stir frequently until pasta is cooked but still firm – about 10 minutes. Serve immediately.

TIME: Preparation takes 15 minutes, cooking takes 1 hour 45 minutes.

Mariner's Salad

*Seafood mixes very well with pasta and the
ingredients can be adapted according to availability.*

SERVES 6

1 lb pasta shells, plain and spinach
4 large scallops, cleaned
1 cup mussels
½ cup lemon juice and water mixed
¾ cup cooked, peeled and de-veined
    shrimp
½ cup clams, cooked
4 oz cooked crab meat, diced
4 green onions, chopped
1 tbsp chopped fresh parsley

Dressing
Grated rind and juice of half a lemon
1 cup mayonnaise
2 tsps paprika
⅓ cup sour cream or plain yogurt
Salt and pepper

1. Cook the pasta for 10 minutes in a large pan of boiling, salted water with 1 tbsp oil. Drain and rinse under hot water. Leave in cold water until ready to use.

2. Cook the scallops and mussels in the lemon juice and water mixture for about 5 minutes, or until fairly firm.

3. Cut the scallops into 2 or 3 pieces, depending upon size.

4. Prepare the dressing and drain the pasta thoroughly.

5. Mix all ingredients together and coat completely with dressing. Stir carefully so that the shellfish do not break-up. Chill for up to 1 hour before serving.

TIME: Preparation takes 25 minutes, cooking takes 15 minutes.

CURRIED SHRIMP SALAD

An unusual salad which is perfect
for a summer lunch.

SERVES 4

2 tbsps olive oil
1 clove garlic, crushed
1 small onion, chopped
1½ tsps curry powder
1 tsp paprika
1 tsp tomato paste
½ cup water
2 slices lemon
Salt and pepper
1 tsp apricot preserve
1 cup mayonnaise
1½ cups small pasta or elbow macaroni
½ lb cooked shrimp, peeled and de-veined
Juice of ½ a lemon

1. Heat oil, and fry garlic and onion gently until soft but not colored. Add curry powder and paprika, and cook for 2 minutes.

2. Stir in tomato paste and water. Add lemon slices, and salt and pepper to taste. Cook slowly for 10 minutes.

3. Stir in the preserve, and bring to a boil, simmering for 2 minutes. Strain and leave to cool. Add mayonnaise.

4. Meanwhile, cook pasta in plenty of boiling salted water for 10 minutes, or until tender, but still firm. Rinse under cold water and drain well.

5. Toss in lemon juice, and put in serving dish. Arrange shrimp on top, and pour over curry sauce. Toss well. Sprinkle with paprika.

TIME: Preparation takes 10 minutes, cooking takes 20 minutes.

PASTA AND VEGETABLES IN PARMESAN DRESSING

Fresh vegetables and pasta in a delicious dressing.

SERVES 6

1 lb pasta spirals or other shapes
½ lb assorted vegetables such as:
Zucchini, cut in rounds or julienne
Broccoli, trimmed into very small florets
Snow peas, ends trimmed
Carrots, cut in rounds or julienne
Celery, cut in julienne
Cucumber, cut in julienne
Green onion, thinly shredded or sliced
Asparagus tips
Green beans, sliced
Red or yellow peppers, thinly sliced

Dressing
½ cup olive oil
3 tbsps lemon juice
1 tbsp sherry
1 tbsp fresh parsley, chopped
1 tbsp fresh basil, chopped, or ½ tbsp dried
¼ cup freshly grated Parmesan cheese
2 tbsps mild mustard
Salt and pepper
Pinch sugar

1. Cook pasta in a large saucepan of boiling, salted water with 1 tbsp oil for 10-12 minutes or until just tender. Rinse under hot water to remove starch. Leave in cold water.

2. Place all the vegetables except the cucumber into boiling salted water for 3 minutes until just tender. Rinse in cold water and leave to drain.

3. Mix the dressing ingredients together very well. Drain the pasta thoroughly and toss with the dressing. Add the vegetables and toss to coat. Refrigerate for up to 1 hour before serving.

TIME: Preparation takes 25 minutes, cooking takes 13-15 minutes.

Italian Pasta Salad

*Buy your favorite Italian cold cuts
for this delicious salad.*

SERVES 4-6

1 lb pasta shapes
½ cup frozen peas
8 oz assorted Italian cold cuts, cut in strips:
    salami, mortadella, prosciutto
4 oz provolone or mozzarella cheese, cut
    in strips
15 black olives, halved and pitted
4 tbsps capers
1 small red onion or 2 shallots, chopped
2 cups oyster mushrooms, stems trimmed
    and sliced

Dressing
3 tbsps white wine vinegar
½ cup olive oil
½ clove garlic, crushed
1 tsp fennel seed, crushed
1 tbsp fresh parsley, chopped
1 tbsp fresh basil, chopped, or ½ tsp dried
1 tbsp prepared mustard
Salt and pepper

1. Put the pasta in a large saucepan of boiling water with a pinch of salt and 1 tbsp oil. Cook for about 10 minutes or until just tender.

2. Add the frozen peas during the last 3 minutes of cooking. Drain the pasta and peas and rinse under hot water. Leave in cold water until ready to use.

3. Mix the dressing ingredients together well.

4. Drain the pasta and peas thoroughly. Mix the pasta and peas with the cold cuts and cheese, olives, capers, chopped onion or shallot and sliced mushrooms.

5. Pour the dressing over the salad and toss all the ingredients together to coat. Do not over-mix.

6. Leave the salad to chill for up to 1 hour before serving.

Time: Preparation takes 25 minutes, cooking takes 10 minutes.

NIÇOISE SALAD

A classic French salad using
Italy's favorite ingredients!

SERVES 4

1½ cups penne

7 oz can tuna, drained and flaked

3 tomatoes, quartered

1 cucumber, cut into julienne

1 cup green beans, cooked

12 black olives, halved, with stones removed

6-8 anchovy fillets, drained, and soaked in milk if desired (see Cook's Tip)

½ cup oil and vinegar dressing

1. Cook penne in plenty of boiling, salted water until tender, but still firm.

2. Rinse in cold water, drain, and leave to dry.

3. Put flaked tuna in the bottom of a salad dish. Toss pasta with tomatoes, cucumber, green beans, olives, and anchovies, and then pour on dressing. Mix together well.

TIME: Preparation takes 15 minutes, cooking takes 15 minutes.

COOK'S TIP: Soaking the anchovy fillets in milk removes any excess salt from the fish. Drain well before using.

Tuna and Tomato Salad

*An economical salad which uses few
ingredients – perfect for unexpected guests.*

SERVES 4

---

1 tbsp chopped fresh basil or marjoram,
   or 1 tsp dried basil or oregano
6 tbsps vinaigrette dressing (see Cook's Tip)
3 cups pasta shells
7 oz can tuna, flaked
6 tomatoes

---

1. Mix herbs with vinaigrette dressing.

2. Cook pasta shells in a large saucepan of boiling salted water until tender – about 10 minutes. Rinse with cold water and drain, shaking off excess water. Toss with 3 tablespoons of vinaigrette dressing. Leave to cool.

3. Meanwhile, slice enough of the tomatoes to arrange around the outside of the serving dish.

4. Chop the rest, pour the remaining vinaigrette dressing over them, and place in the center of the dish.

5. Add tuna to the pasta shells, and toss gently. Serve in the center of the dish over the chopped tomatoes.

TIME: Preparation takes 10 minutes, cooking takes 15 minutes.

COOK'S TIP: To make your own vinaigrette dressing, mix 4½ tbsps olive oil with 1½ tbsps white wine vinegar, a pinch of salt and pepper and about ⅛-¼ tsp of prepared mustard.

Mexican Chicken Salad

A simple salad which is both quick and tasty.

SERVES 4

1¼ cups pasta shells
2 cups cooked chicken, shredded
7 oz can corn, drained
1 celery stalk, sliced
1 red pepper, diced
1 green pepper, diced

Dressing
1 tbsp mayonnaise
2 tbsps vinegar
Salt and pepper

1. Cook pasta in plenty of boiling salted water until just tender. Drain well and leave to cool.

2. Meanwhile, combine mayonnaise with vinegar and salt and pepper to taste.

3. When the pasta has cooled, add chicken, corn, celery and peppers.

4. Toss together well and serve with the dressing.

TIME: Preparation takes 10 minutes, cooking takes 15 minutes.

131

GIANFOTTERE SALAD

Eggplant, zucchini and peppers are
combined with pasta in this simple salad.

SERVES 4

1 eggplant
2 tomatoes
1 zucchini
1 red pepper
1 green pepper
1 onion
4 tbsps olive oil
1 clove garlic
Salt and pepper
1 lb whole wheat pasta spirals or bows

1. Cut eggplant into ½ inch slices. Sprinkle with salt and set aside for 30 minutes.

2. Peel the tomatoes – put them into boiling water for 20 seconds, rinse in cold water, and peel the skins off. Chop coarsely.

3. Cut zucchini into ½ inch slices. Chop the peppers coarsely.

4. Chop the onion and garlic.

5. Heat 3 tbsps olive oil in pan and fry onion gently until transparent.

6. Meanwhile, rinse salt from eggplant, and pat dry with paper towels. Chop coarsely.

7. Add eggplant, zucchini, peppers, tomatoes and garlic to onion, and fry gently for 20 minutes. Season with salt and pepper. Allow to cool.

8. Meanwhile, cook pasta spirals in plenty of boiling, salted water for 10 minutes, or until tender but still firm. Rinse in cold water and drain well. Toss in the remaining 1 tbsp olive oil.

9. Toss vegetables together with pasta spirals.

TIME: *Preparation takes 40 minutes, cooking takes 30 minutes.*

ZUCCHINI SALAD

*Raw vegetables are full of vitamins, and raw zucchini in particular
has the added advantage of having a delicious taste and texture.*

SERVES 4

½ lb macaroni
4 tomatoes
4-5 zucchini, sliced thinly
8 stuffed green olives, sliced
6 tbsps vinaigrette dressing (see Cook's Tip)

1. Put the macaroni into a large saucepan
and cover with boiling water. Add a little
salt and simmer for 10 minutes, or until
tender but still firm. Rinse in cold water
and drain well.

2. Cut a small cross in the tops of each
tomato and plunge into boiling water for
30 seconds.

3. Carefully remove the skins from the
blanched tomatoes, using a sharp knife.
Chop the tomatoes coarsely.

4. Mix all the ingredients in a large bowl
and chill in the refrigerator for 30 minutes
before serving.

TIME: Preparation takes 15 minutes, cooking takes about 10 minutes.

VARIATION: Use any other pasta shape of your choice.

COOK'S TIP: To make your own vinaigrette dressing, mix 4½ tbsps olive oil with 1½ tbsps
white wine vinegar, a pinch of salt and pepper and about ⅛-¼ tsp of prepared mustard.

TUNA AND PASTA WITH RED KIDNEY BEANS

The perfect summer salad for lunch or a light dinner.

SERVES 4-6

1½ cups small pasta shells
8 oz can red kidney beans, drained
   and rinsed
1 cup small mushrooms, quartered
14 oz can tuna, drained and flaked
4 green onions, sliced
2 tbsps mixed fresh herbs chopped, or
   1 tbsp dried

Dressing
½ cup olive oil
3 tbsps white wine vinegar
Squeeze of lemon juice
1 tbsp Dijon mustard
Salt and pepper

1. Cook the pasta shells in boiling, salted water with 1 tbsp oil for 10 minutes or until just tender. Rinse under hot water and then place in cold water until ready to use.

2. Mix the dressing ingredients together thoroughly.

3. Drain the pasta shells. Mix the pasta with the beans, mushrooms, tuna, green onions and herbs.

4. Pour over the dressing and toss to coat. Chill up to 1 hour in the refrigerator before serving.

TIME: Preparation takes 20 minutes, cooking takes 10 minutes.

SPAGHETTI AMATRICIANA

This is another quickly cooked sauce with a rich spicy taste.
Reduce the amount of chili pepper for a less fiery flavor.

SERVES 4

1 onion
6 slices Canadian bacon
1 lb ripe tomatoes
1 red chili pepper, diced
1½ tbsps oil
12 oz spaghetti
Parmesan cheese (optional)

1. Slice the onion thinly. Cut the bacon into thin strips.

2. Drop the tomatoes into boiling water for 6-8 seconds. Remove with a draining spoon, place in cold water, and leave to cool completely. This will make the skin easier to remove.

3. Peel the tomatoes, cut them in half and remove the seeds and pulp with a teaspoon. Rub the seeds and pulp through a strainer and retain juice to use in the sauce if desired. Chop the tomato flesh roughly and set it aside.

4. Heat the oil in a sauté pan and add the onion and bacon. Stir over medium heat for about 5 minutes, until the onion is transparent. Drain off excess fat, add the tomatoes and pepper, and mix well. Simmer the sauce gently, uncovered, for about 5 minutes, stirring occasionally.

5. Meanwhile, cook the spaghetti in boiling, salted water with 1 tbsp oil for about 10-12 minutes. Drain and rinse in hot water and toss in a colander to dry. To serve, spoon the sauce on top of the spaghetti and sprinkle with freshly grated Parmesan cheese, if desired.

TIME: Preparation takes about 20-25 minutes, cooking takes about 10-12 minutes for the spaghetti and about 8 minutes for the sauce.

PASTA SPIRALS WITH CREAMY PARSLEY SAUCE

Serve this quick and easy dish with French bread for the perfect mid-week dinner.

SERVES 3-4

2 tbsps butter or margarine
1 tbsp flour
1 cup milk
9 oz pasta spirals
1 tbsp chopped fresh parsley
1 tbsp lemon juice or 1 tsp vinegar

1. Heat butter in pan; when melted, stir in flour. Heat gently for 1 minute. Remove from heat, and gradually stir in milk. Return to heat, and stir continuously until boiling. Cook for 2 minutes.

2. Meanwhile, cook pasta spirals in plenty of boiling, salted water for 10 minutes, or until tender, but still firm. Rinse in hot water, and drain well.

3. Just before serving, add parsley and lemon juice to sauce, and pour over pasta. Serve immediately.

TIME: Preparation takes 5 minutes, cooking takes 15 minutes.

TORTIGLIONI ALLA PUTTANESCA

*Anchovy fillets add a special flavor
to this classic Italian dish.*

SERVES 4

---

7 oz can plum tomatoes, drained
6-8 anchovy fillets
10 oz tortiglioni (pasta spirals)
2 tbsps olive oil
2 cloves garlic, crushed
½ tsp fresh or pinch dried basil
Pinch chili powder
½ cup black olives, pitted and chopped
2 tbsps chopped fresh parsley
Salt and pepper

---

1. Chop tomatoes and anchovies.

2. Cook pasta in plenty of boiling salted water for 10 minutes, or until tender but still firm. Rinse in hot water and drain. Pour into a warmed bowl.

3. Meanwhile, heat oil in pan, add garlic, basil and chili powder, and cook for 1 minute.

4. Add tomatoes, olives, parsley and anchovies, and cook for a few minutes.

5. Season with salt and pepper. Pour sauce over pasta and mix together thoroughly. Serve immediately.

TIME: Preparation takes 10 minutes, cooking takes 15 minutes.

PASTA SHELLS WITH MUSHROOM SAUCE

This adaptable dish can be served for lunch or dinner.

SERVES 3-4

½ lb mushrooms
2 tbsps butter or margarine
1 tbsp flour
1 cup milk
Salt and pepper
10 oz pasta shells

1. Rinse the mushrooms and chop them coarsely.

2. Melt butter in a saucepan and add mushrooms. Fry for 5 minutes, stirring occasionally. Stir in the flour and cook for 1 minute.

3. Reduce the heat, and add milk gradually, stirring continuously. Bring to a boil and cook for 3 minutes. Season with salt and pepper.

4. Meanwhile, cook the pasta shells in plenty of boiling salted water for 10 minutes, or until tender, but still firm.

5. Rinse in hot water and drain well. Place in a warmed serving dish, and pour over mushroom sauce. Serve immediately.

TIME: Preparation takes 5 minutes, cooking takes 15 minutes.

TAGLIATELLE WITH CREAMY LIVER SAUCE

Chicken livers are lovely mixed with cream and mushrooms;
add pasta to the mixture and you have the perfect mid-week treat.

SERVES 3-4

3 tbsps olive oil
2 medium onions, sliced
1 clove garlic, crushed
¾ cup mushrooms, sliced
1 lb chicken livers, cleaned and sliced
⅓ cup heavy cream
2 eggs, beaten
Salt and pepper
10 oz tagliatelle
1 tbsp chopped fresh parsley

1. Melt 2 tbsps of the oil in a large frying pan and cook onions and garlic gently until softened.

2. Add mushrooms and cook for 3 minutes. Add chicken livers, and cook until lightly browned. Remove from heat and stir in cream. Return to low heat and cook, uncovered, for another 2 minutes.

3. Remove from heat and stir in lightly beaten eggs. Season with salt and pepper to taste.

4. Meanwhile, cook the tagliatelle in plenty of boiling, salted water for 10 minutes, or until tender but still firm, stirring occasionally.

5. Drain tagliatelle, toss in remaining oil, and black pepper. Serve sauce over tagliatelle and sprinkle with parsley.

TIME: Preparation takes 10 minutes, cooking takes 15 minutes.

SPAGHETTI WITH TOMATO, SALAMI AND GREEN OLIVES

*Vary the quantities of salami and green olives
in this recipe according to your taste.*

SERVES 2-3

14 oz can plum tomatoes
⅓ lb salami, sliced and shredded
1 cup green olives, stoned and chopped
½ tbsp dried oregano
Salt and pepper
10 oz spaghetti
2 tbsps olive oil
1 clove garlic, crushed
¼ cup pecorino cheese, grated

1. Purée tomatoes in a blender or food processor and put into a saucepan. Add oregano, olives and salami and heat gently. Add salt and pepper to taste.

2. Meanwhile, cook spaghetti in plenty of boiling, salted water for 10 minutes, or until tender but still firm. Drain well.

3. Heat olive oil in the pan used to cook the spaghetti, and add garlic and freshly-ground black pepper.

4. Add spaghetti and pour the sauce over. Toss well. Serve immediately with pecorino cheese.

TIME: Preparation takes 15 minutes, cooking takes 15 minutes.

MACARONI CHEESE WITH HOT DOGS

Kids and adults alike will love this delicious, filling meal.

SERVES 4

8 hot dogs
1 lb macaroni
¼ cup butter or margarine
¾ cup all-purpose flour
2 cups milk
1½ cups cheddar cheese, grated
1 tsp dry mustard
Salt and pepper

Garnish
½ red pepper, cut into thin strips

1. Poach the hot dogs for 5-8 minutes. Remove skins and, when cold, cut into diagonal slices.

2. Cook macaroni in plenty of boiling salted water for about 10 minutes, or until tender but still firm. Rinse in hot water and drain well.

3. Meanwhile, melt the butter in a pan. Stir in the flour and cook gently for 1 minute. Reduce heat and gradually add milk, stirring all the time. Bring to a boil, stirring continuously, reduce heat and cook gently for 3 minutes.

4. Add hot dogs, grated cheese, mustard, and salt and pepper to taste. Stir well.

5. Add macaroni and mix in well. Pour mixture into an oven-proof dish and sprinkle the remaining cheese over the top.

6. Make a lattice of pepper, and cook under a preheated broiler until golden brown. Serve immediately.

TIME: Preparation takes 10 minutes, cooking takes 20 minutes.

Spirali with Spinach and Bacon

Pasta doesn't have to have a sauce that cooks for hours. This whole dish takes about 15 minutes. True Italian "fast food!"

SERVES 4

12 oz pasta spirals
8 oz fresh spinach
3 oz bacon
1 small red or green chili pepper
1 small red pepper
1 small onion
1 clove garlic, crushed
3 tbsps olive oil
Salt and pepper

1. Cook the pasta in boiling, salted water for about 10-12 minutes or until just tender. Drain the pasta in a colander and rinse it under hot water. Keep the pasta in a bowl of water until ready to use.

2. Tear the stalks off the spinach and wash the leaves well in the water several times. Set aside to drain.

3. Dice the bacon finely. Slice the chili and the red pepper finely. Slice the onion thinly.

4. Roll up several of the spinach leaves into a cigar shape and then shred them finely. Repeat until all the spinach is shredded.

5. Heat the oil in a sauté pan and add garlic, onion, peppers and bacon. Fry for 2 minutes, add the spinach and fry for another 2 minutes, stirring continuously. Season with salt and pepper.

6. Drain the pasta spirals and toss them in a colander to remove excess water. Mix with the spinach sauce and serve immediately.

TIME: Preparation takes 20 minutes, cooking takes about 15 minutes.

PENNE WITH HAM AND ASPARAGUS

*The Italian word penne means quills, due to the
diagonal cut on both ends.*

SERVES 4

8 oz penne
12 oz fresh asparagus
4 oz cooked ham
2 tbsps butter or margarine
1 cup heavy cream
Parmesan cheese (optional)

1. Trim asparagus spears about 1 inch from the bottom.

2. Cut the ham into strips about ½-inch thick.

3. Steam the asparagus spears for about 2 minutes. Drain and allow to cool.

4. Cut the asparagus into 1 inch lengths, leaving the tips whole.

5. Melt the butter in the sauté pan and add the asparagus and ham. Cook briefly to evaporate the liquid and then add the cream. Bring to a boil and cook for about 5 minutes to thicken the cream.

6. Meanwhile, cook the pasta in boiling salted water with 1 tbsp oil for about 10-12 minutes.

7. Drain the pasta and rinse under hot water. Toss in a colander to drain and mix with the sauce. Serve with grated Parmesan cheese, if desired.

TIME: Preparation takes about 20 minutes, cooking takes 10-12 minutes for the pasta and 8 minutes for the sauce.

155

HOMEMADE TAGLIATELLE WITH SUMMER SAUCE

Pasta making is not as difficult as you might think. It is well worth it, too, because homemade pasta is in a class by itself.

SERVES 4

Pasta Dough
1 cup all-purpose flour
1 cup bread flour
2 large eggs
2 tsps olive oil
Pinch salt

Sauce
1 lb unpeeled tomatoes, seeded and diced
1 large green pepper, diced
1 onion, diced
1 tbsp fresh basil, chopped, or ½ tsp dried
1 tbsp fresh parsley, chopped
2 cloves garlic, crushed
½ cup olive oil and vegetable oil, mixed

1. Combine all the sauce ingredients, mixing well. Cover and refrigerate overnight.

2. Place the flours in a mound on a work surface and make a well in the center. Place the eggs, oil and salt in the center of the well.

3. Using a fork, beat the ingredients in the center to blend them and gradually incorporate the flour from the outside edge. The dough may also be mixed in a food processor.

4. When half the flour is incorporated, start kneading using the palms of the hands until all the flour is incorporated. This may also be done in a food processor. Cover the dough and leave it to rest for 15 minutes.

5. Divide the dough in quarters and roll out thinly with a rolling pin on a floured surface, dusting dough lightly with flour before rolling. If using a pasta machine, following the manufacturer's directions. Allow the sheets of pasta to dry for about 10 minutes on a floured surface or tea towels. Cut the sheets into strips about ¼ inch wide by hand or machine, dusting lightly with flour while cutting. Leave the cut pasta to dry for 5-10 minutes.

6. Cook the pasta for 5-6 minutes in boiling, salted water with a spoonful of oil. Drain the pasta and rinse under very hot water. Toss in a colander to drain excess water. Place the hot pasta in serving dish. Pour the cold sauce over and toss well.

TIME: Preparation takes about 30 minutes, cooking takes about 5-6 minutes.

Pasta with Fresh Tomato and Basil Sauce

Pasta is a good addition to a healthy diet, as it is very filling and can be served with a variety of low calorie sauces.

SERVES 4-6

1 small onion, finely chopped
1 lb fresh tomatoes
2 tbsps tomato paste
1 orange
2 cloves garlic, crushed
Salt and freshly ground black pepper
½ cup red wine
½ cup chicken stock
2 tbsps coarsely chopped fresh basil
12 oz whole wheat pasta

1. Finely chop the onion.

2. Cut a small cross in the tops of the tomatoes and plunge them into boiling water for 30 seconds. Remove the tomatoes from the water and carefully peel away the loosened skin.

3. Cut the tomatoes into quarters, and remove and discard the seeds. Chop the tomato flesh coarsely, and put this, the onion and the tomato paste into a large saucepan.

4. Heat the onion and tomatoes over a gentle heat, stirring continuously until the tomatoes soften and begin to lose their juice.

5. Finely grate the orange rind. Cut the orange in half and squeeze out the juice.

6. Add the orange rind and juice to the large saucepan along with all the remaining ingredients except the pasta, and bring to a boil.

7. Continue to boil until the sauce has reduced and thickened, and the vegetables are soft.

8. While the sauce is cooking, put the pasta into another saucepan with enough boiling water to cover. Season with a little salt and cook for 10-15 minutes, or until the pasta is soft.

9. Drain the pasta in a colander and stir it into the hot sauce.

10. Serve at once with salad.

TIME: Preparation takes 15-20 minutes, cooking takes 10-15 minutes.

VARIATION: Add 1 cup thinly sliced mushrooms to the sauce.

LASAGNE WITH FOUR CHEESES

*Adapt this dish by using your own
favorite Italian cheeses.*

SERVES 2-3

1 tbsp olive oil
½ lb green lasagne
¼ cup butter
3 tbsps all-purpose flour
3¼ cups milk
6 tbsps grated Parmesan cheese
¼ cup grated gruyére cheese
¼ cup mozzarella, diced
¼ cup pecorino, diced
Salt, pepper and nutmeg

1. Fill a large pan with salted water. Add the olive oil. Cook the lasagne 4 or 5 sheets at a time for 7-10 minutes. Lift each batch out carefully and plunge into cold water. When all the pasta has been cooked, drain well on absorbent paper.

2. Melt the butter over gentle heat. When melted, add the flour and mix well. Heat the mixture gently until it turns a pale straw color. Stir in the milk gradually, stirring constantly until thick. Add the cheeses to the sauce, reserving 2 tbsps Parmesan. Season with salt, pepper and nutmeg.

3. Stir until the cheeses have melted.

4. Butter a deep baking dish generously. Add alternate layers of lasagne and sauce – there should be at least four layers. Finish with a layer of sauce, and sprinkle with the reserved grated Parmesan. Cook at 350°F for 45 minutes until bubbling and golden brown.

TIME: Preparation takes 15-20 minutes, cooking takes 45 minutes.

MEAT RAVIOLI WITH RED PEPPER SAUCE

Pepper-flavored pasta dough is rolled thinly, cut into squares, filled with a delicious meat stuffing and served with a creamy red pepper sauce.

SERVES 4

2 red peppers, seeded
1¾ cups all-purpose flour, sifted
2 eggs
1 cup ground beef
1 tbsp fresh parsley, finely chopped
½ onion, chopped
½ cup light cream
½ cup butter
Salt and pepper

1. Place the red peppers in a food processor and blend until liquid. Place in a small bowl and set aside, giving time for the pulp to rise to the surface. This takes approximately 30 minutes.

2. To make the dough, place the sifted flour in a bowl with a pinch of salt. Add 1 egg and 3 tbsps of the pepper pulp (not the juice).

3. Mix together really well and form into a ball. Set the dough aside for 30 minutes.

4. Mix together the meat, parsley and onion, and season with salt and pepper.

5. Roll the dough out very thinly, using a pasta machine if available, and cut into small squares. Place a little stuffing on half of the cut squares. Beat the remaining egg and brush the edges of the squares with the egg. Cover with another square of dough and seal the edges by pinching together with your fingers.

6. Bring a large saucepan of salted water to a boil and cook the ravioli for approximately 3 minutes – longer if you prefer your pasta well cooked.

7. While the ravioli are cooking, prepare the sauce by heating the cream with ½ cup of the red pepper pulp. Bring to a boil and then whisk in the butter.

8. Drain the ravioli and then pat them dry with a tea towel. Serve with the hot cream sauce.

TIME: Preparation takes about 50 minutes, resting time is 30 minutes and cooking time approximately 15 minutes.

VARIATION: Add a little wine vinegar (1 tsp) and a few drops of Tabasco to the sauce to give it a slightly peppery taste.

WATCHPOINT: When rolling out the dough, flour it well so that it does not stick to the rolling pin or pasta machine rollers.

SPAGHETTI WITH CRAB AND BACON

This recipe includes a wonderful preparation of home-made parsley pasta.
It is tossed and served with a seafood sauce, crab and bacon.

SERVES 4-6

1 bunch parsley (approximately 6 tbsps)
4¼ cups all-purpose flour
4 eggs
8 oz bacon
1 tbsp olive oil
¾ lb crab meat, chopped
1½ cups heavy cream
3 tbsps butter
Fresh chervil, optional
Salt and pepper

1. Trim the leaves off the parsley, discard the stalks. Cook for 10 minutes in boiling water. Pass through a fine sieve and reserve the cooking liquid.

2. Purée the parsley with 3 tbsps of the cooking liquid in a blender.

3. In a bowl, mix together the flour, salt, eggs and 1½ tbsps parsley purée. Form into a ball.

4. Quarter the dough and form these pieces into balls. Press each ball flat and run it through a pasta machine, or roll out with a rolling pin.

5. Thin the dough progressively by passing it through the machine several times. Flour the dough frequently throughout the operation.

6. Run the flattened strips of dough through the spaghetti cutter or cut with a knife.

7. Cut the bacon first into strips and then into small rectangles.

8. Add the olive oil to boiling, salted water and cook the spaghetti for 5 minutes. Strain and rinse.

9. Break up the crab meat into small pieces with your fingers.

10. Heat the cream gently with the crab and bacon pieces.

11. Meanwhile, heat the butter in a pan and when it bubbles, add the spaghetti (first reheated by plunging for 30 seconds in boiling water). Mix well and season with salt and pepper.

12. Place the buttered spaghetti around the edges of the dinner plates and arrange the crab/bacon mixture in the center. Garnish with the fresh chervil.

TIME: Preparation takes 1 hour, cooking takes 20 minutes.

Cook's Tip: If you do not wish to prepare the spaghetti yourself you can buy fresh spaghetti, either parsley or plain verde, at a delicatessen or supermarket.

TAGLIATELLE WITH BLUE CHEESE

Fruit and cheese marries well to give a sweet and savory dish.

SERVES 6

4¼ cups all-purpose flour
5 eggs
1 tbsp olive oil
4 oz blue cheese (roquefort or stilton)
1 cup dried apricots
1¼ cups heavy cream
¼ cup milk
¼ cup pine nuts
½ bunch chives
Salt and pepper

1. In a bowl, work together the flour, a pinch of salt and eggs to form a soft ball of dough.

2. Quarter the dough and flatten each piece. Coat each piece with plenty of flour. Flour the rollers of a pasta machine and pass the dough through the machine, or roll it out with a rolling pin.

3. Continue rolling the pasta until thin. Flour frequently during the process.

4. Thread the dough strips through the tagliatelle cutter or cut into strips with a knife. Dredge the noodles with flour and allow to dry for 2 hours.

5. Bring to a boil a saucepan of salted water with 1 tbsp oil. Cook the pasta for 2 to 4 minutes, stirring with a fork.

6. Drain the tagliatelle and rinse in plenty of cold water to prevent sticking. Set aside.

7. Break up the cheese and force through a sieve with the back of a spoon.

8. Cut the apricots into strips, then dice.

9. Slowly heat the cream in a saucepan. Stir in the cheese and milk. Blend until smooth with a hand-held electric blender.

10. While the sauce is hot, stir in the tagliatelle and apricots, and season as necessary. Heat through quickly so the cream does not curdle or the noodles overcook.

11. Mix the pasta with two forks. Remove from the heat and mix in the pine nuts.

12. Chop the chives finely and sprinkle them over the tagliatelle; serve immediately.

TIME: Preparation takes 1 hour, cooking takes 16 minutes. Drying the pasta takes 2 hours.

PASTA WITH LEEKS AND MUSSELS

*An easy pasta dish to prepare, ideal
for unexpected guests.*

SERVES 6

1 lb mussels
½ cup white wine
1 shallot, chopped
2 medium-sized leeks
¾ cup heavy cream
1 lb spiral-shaped pasta
1 tbsp oil
2 slices ham
1½ tbsps butter
Fresh chives to garnish
Salt and pepper

1. Scrub the mussels; remove the beards and wash in several changes of water to remove any sand.

2. In a large, covered saucepan, cook the mussels in the white wine with the chopped shallot for approximately 5 minutes, over a high heat.

3. Cool and remove the opened mussels from their shells. Reserve the cooking liquid.

4. Quarter each leek lengthwise, wash thoroughly and slice finely.

5. In a covered saucepan, cook the leeks in the cream, with salt and pepper to taste, for 10 minutes over a low heat.

6. In a large saucepan of boiling water, cook the pasta with 1 tbsp oil. Stir the pasta as it cooks, to prevent sticking.

7. Drain after 5 or 6 minutes. Rinse in cold water to prevent sticking.

8. Slice the ham into small pieces.

9. Strain the mussel cooking liquid through a sieve lined with cheesecloth. Measure out approximately ½ cup.

10. Add the shelled mussels and the mussel liquid to the cream mixture, and cook for 4 minutes, stirring constantly.

11. Melt the butter in a deep frying pan and reheat the pasta gently with the ham. Season to taste.

12. When the pasta is heated through, add the cream and leek sauce, and serve garnished with the chopped chives.

TIME: Preparation takes 30 minutes, cooking takes 25 minutes.

FISH RAVIOLI

This recipe has quite a few ingredients but it is not too difficult to prepare and the end result tastes wonderful.

SERVES 4

Dough
1¼ cups bread flour
Pinch of salt
3 eggs

Filling
½ lb sole or flounder fillets
1 slice of onion
1 slice of lemon
6 peppercorns
1 bay leaf
1 tbsp lemon juice
1 cup water
2 eggs, beaten
2 tbsps bread crumbs
1 green onion, finely chopped

Lemon sauce
2 tbsps butter or margarine
2 tbsps flour
1 cup strained cooking liquid from fish
2 tbsps heavy cream
2 tbsps lemon juice
Salt and pepper

Filling
1. Preheat oven to 350°F.

2. Wash and dry fish. Place in oven-proof dish with slice of onion, slice of lemon, peppercorns, bay leaf, lemon juice and water. Cover and cook for 20 minutes.

3. Remove fish from liquid and allow to drain. Strain liquid and set aside. When fish is cool, beat with the back of a spoon to a pulp.

4. Add eggs, bread crumbs and green onion, and salt and pepper to taste. Mix well.

Dough
1. Sift flour and salt into a bowl. Make a well in the center, and add the eggs. Work the flour and eggs together with a spoon, and then knead by hand until a smooth dough is formed. Leave to rest for 15 minutes.

2. Lightly flour a pastry board and roll out dough thinly into a rectangle. Cut dough in half.

3. Shape the filling into small balls and set them about 1½ inches apart on one half of the dough. Place the other half of the dough on top and cut with a ravioli cutter or small pastry cutter. Seal the edges.

4. Cook in batches in a large pan with plenty of boiling, salted water until tender – about 8 minutes. Remove carefully with a slotted spoon. Meanwhile, make sauce.

Sauce
1. Melt butter in a pan. Stir in flour and cook gently for 30 seconds. Reduce the heat and gradually stir in liquid from cooked fish. Return to heat and bring to a boil. Simmer for 4 minutes, stirring continuously.

2. Add cream and mix well. Season to taste. Remove from heat and gradually stir in lemon juice and seasoning. Do not reboil. Pour sauce over ravioli and serve immediately.

TIME: Preparation takes 30 minutes, cooking takes 30 minutes.

PASTITSIO

*This is like an Italian version of Shepherd's Pie
with macaroni instead of potato.*

SERVES 4

8 oz macaroni
4 tbsps butter or margarine
¼ cup Parmesan cheese, grated
Pinch of grated nutmeg
2 eggs, beaten
1 medium onion, chopped
1 clove garlic, crushed
1 lb ground beef
2 tbsps tomato paste
¼ cup red wine
½ cup beef stock
2 tbsps chopped fresh parsley
2 tbsps all-purpose flour
½ cup milk
Salt
Pepper

1. Preheat oven to 375°F.

2. Cook macaroni in plenty of boiling, salted water for 10 minutes, or until tender but still firm. Rinse under hot water. Drain.

3. Put one-third of the butter in the pan and return macaroni to it. Add half the cheese, nutmeg, and salt and pepper to taste. Leave to cool. Mix in half the beaten egg and put aside.

4. Melt half of the remaining butter in a pan and fry the onion and garlic gently until onion is soft. Increase temperature, add meat, and fry until browned.

5. Add tomato paste, stock, parsley and wine, and season with salt and pepper. Simmer for 20 minutes.

6. In a small pan, melt the rest of the butter. Stir in the flour and cook for 30 seconds. Remove from heat and stir in milk. Bring to a boil, stirring continuously, until the sauce thickens.

7. Beat in the remaining egg and season to taste. Spoon half the macaroni into a serving dish and cover with the meat sauce.

8. Put on another layer of macaroni and smooth over. Pour over white sauce, sprinkle with remaining cheese, and bake in the oven for 30 minutes until golden brown. Serve immediately.

TIME: Preparation takes 10 minutes, cooking takes 1 hour.

Tortellini

*Vary the amount of Parmesan cheese in
this recipe to suit your own taste.*

SERVES 4

Dough
1¼ cups bread flour
Pinch of salt
1 tbsp water
1 tbsp oil
3 eggs

Filling
2 tbsps cream cheese
1 cooked chicken breast, finely diced
2 tbsps ham, finely diced
2 spinach leaves, stalks removed, cooked
  and chopped finely
1 tbsp grated Parmesan cheese
1 egg, beaten
Salt and pepper

Sauce
1 cup heavy cream
¼ lb mushrooms, cleaned and sliced
¼ cup Parmesan cheese, grated
1 tbsp chopped fresh parsley
Salt and pepper

Filling

1. Beat the cream cheese until soft and smooth. Add chicken, ham, spinach and Parmesan cheese, and mix well. Add egg gradually, and salt and pepper to taste. Set aside.

Dough

1. Sift flour and salt onto a board. Make a well in the center. Mix water, oil and lightly beaten eggs together, and gradually pour into well, working in the flour with the other hand, a little at a time. Continue until the mixture comes together in a firm ball of dough.

2. Knead on a lightly-floured board for 5 minutes, or until smooth and elastic. Put into a bowl, cover with a cloth, and leave to stand for 15 minutes.

3. Roll dough out on a lightly-floured board as thinly as possible. Using a 2 inch cutter, cut out circles. Put ½ teaspoon of filling into the center of each circle. Fold in half, pressing edges together firmly. Wrap around forefinger, and press ends together. Cook in batches in a large pan, in plenty of boiling salted water for about 10 minutes until tender, stirring occasionally.

Sauce

1. Meanwhile, gently heat cream in a pan. Add mushrooms, Parmesan cheese, parsley, and salt and pepper to taste. Gently cook for 3 minutes.

To serve, toss sauce together with tortellini and sprinkle with parsley.

Time: Preparation takes 30 minutes, cooking takes 15 minutes.

MEAT RAVIOLI

*Preparing your own pasta dough is very satisfying as it
almost always tastes better than packaged varieties.*

SERVES 4

Dough
1¼ cups bread flour
Pinch of salt
3 eggs

Filling
4 tbsps butter or margarine
1 clove garlic, crushed
1 onion, grated
½ lb ground beef
½ cup red wine
Salt and pepper
2 tbsps bread crumbs
½ cup cooked spinach, chopped
2 eggs, beaten

Sauce
14 oz can plum tomatoes
1 small onion, grated
1 small carrot, diced finely
1 bay leaf
3 parsley stalks
Salt and pepper
½ cup Parmesan cheese, grated

Filling
1. Heat butter in a frying pan. Add garlic
and onion, and fry gently for 1 minute.
Add ground beef and fry until browned.
Add red wine, and salt and pepper to
taste, and cook, uncovered, for 15 minutes.

2. Strain juices and reserve them for the
sauce. Allow to cool.

3. Add bread crumbs, chopped spinach,
and beaten eggs to bind.

4. Adjust salt and pepper to taste.

Dough
1. Sift flour in a bowl with salt. Make a
well in the center and add the eggs. Work
flour and eggs together with a spoon, then
knead by hand, until a smooth dough is
formed. Leave dough to rest for 15 minutes.

2. Lightly flour board, and roll out dough
thinly into a rectangle. Cut dough in half.

3. Shape the filling into small balls, and
set them about 1½ inches apart on one
half of the dough.

4. Place the other half of dough on top
and cut with a ravioli cutter or small
pastry cutter. Seal the edges by pinching
together or pressing with a fork.

5. Cook in batches in a large, wide pan
with plenty of boiling, salted water until
tender – about 8 minutes. Remove
carefully with a slotted spoon. Meanwhile,
make the sauce.

Sauce
1. Put all the sauce ingredients in a
saucepan. Add juice from cooked meat
and bring to a boil. Simmer for 10
minutes. Push through a sieve, and return
smooth sauce to pan. Adjust seasoning.

To serve, put ravioli in a warm dish and
cover with tomato sauce. Serve immediately,
sprinkled with grated Parmesan cheese.

TIME: Preparation takes 30 minutes, cooking takes 5 minutes.

FETTUCINE ESCARGOTS WITH LEEKS AND SUN-DRIED TOMATOES

These dried tomatoes keep for a long time and allow you to add a sunny taste to dishes whatever the time of year.

SERVES 4-6

6 sun-dried tomatoes
14 oz can escargots (snails), drained
12 oz fresh or dried whole wheat fettucine
3 tbsps olive oil
2 cloves garlic, crushed
1 large or 2 small leeks, trimmed, split, well washed and finely sliced
6 oyster, shittake or other large mushrooms
4 tbsps chicken or vegetable stock
3 tbsps dry white wine
6 tbsps heavy cream
2 tsps fresh basil, chopped
2 tsps fresh parsley, chopped
Salt and pepper

1. Drain the escargots well and dry with paper towels.

2. Place the fettucine in boiling salted water and cook for about 10-12 minutes, or until al dente. Drain, rinse under hot water and leave in a colander to drain dry.

3. Meanwhile, heat the olive oil in a frying pan and add the garlic and leeks. Cook slowly to soften slightly. Add the mushrooms and cook until the leeks are tender crisp. Remove to a plate. Add the drained escargots to the pan and cook over high heat for about 2 minutes, stirring constantly.

4. Pour on the stock and wine and bring to a boil. Boil to reduce by about a quarter and add the cream and tomatoes. Bring to a boil then cook slowly for about 3 minutes. Add the herbs, and salt and pepper to taste.

5. Add the leeks, mushrooms and fettucine to the pan and heat through. Serve immediately.

TIME: Preparation takes about 15-20 minutes.

LASAGNE NAPOLETANA

This is a lasagne as it is cooked and eaten in Naples.
With its layer of red, green and white it looks as delicious
as it tastes and is very easy to prepare.

SERVES 6

9 sheets spinach lasagne pasta
1 tbsp olive oil

Tomato Sauce

2 tbsps olive oil
2 cloves garlic, crushed
2 lbs fresh tomatoes, peeled, or canned
    tomatoes, drained
2 tbsps fresh basil, chopped, or 1 tbsp
    dried
Salt and pepper
Pinch sugar
6 whole basil leaves to garnish

Cheese filling

1 lb ricotta cheese
4 tbsps unsalted butter
2 cups Mozzarella cheese, grated
Salt and pepper
Pinch nutmeg

1. Cook the pasta for 8 minutes in boiling salted water with 1 tbsp oil. Drain and rinse under hot water and place in a single layer on a damp cloth. Cover with another damp cloth and set aside.

2. To prepare the sauce, cook the garlic in oil for about 1 minute in a large saucepan. When pale brown, add the tomatoes, basil, salt, pepper and sugar. (If using fresh tomatoes, drop into boiling water for 6-8 seconds. Transfer to cold water and leave to cool completely. This will make the skin easier to remove.)

3. Lower the heat and simmer the sauce for 35 minutes. Add more seasoning or sugar to taste.

4. Beat the ricotta cheese and butter together until creamy and stir into the remaining filling ingredients.

5. To assemble the lasagne, oil a rectangular baking dish and place 3 sheets of lasagne on the base. Cover with one third of the sauce and carefully spread on a layer of cheese. Place another 3 layers of pasta over the cheese and cover with another third of the sauce. Add the remaining cheese filling and cover with the remaining pasta. Spoon the remaining sauce on top.

6. Cover with foil and bake for 20 minutes at 375°F. Uncover and cook for 10 minutes longer. Garnish with the fresh basil leaves (if available) and leave to stand for 10-15 minutes before serving.

TIME: Preparation takes about 25 minutes, cooking takes about 1-1¼ hours.

ITALIAN CASSEROLE

*Serve this hearty main course with a
green salad or broccoli, and fresh bread.*

SERVES 4

1 cup small macaroni
2 tbsps butter or margarine
1 clove garlic, crushed
1 onion, chopped
2 16 oz cans plum tomatoes
1 tbsp tomato paste
1 red pepper, chopped coarsely
1 green pepper, chopped coarsely
½ lb salami, cut into chunks
10 pitted black olives, halved
½ lb mozzarella cheese, sliced thinly
Salt and pepper

1. Cook the macaroni in plenty of boiling salted water for 10 minutes, or until tender but still firm. Rinse under hot water and drain well. Place in a shallow, oven-proof dish.

2. Meanwhile, heat butter in pan, and fry onion and garlic gently until soft.

3. Add undrained tomatoes, tomato paste, red and green peppers, salami and olives, and stir well. Simmer uncovered for 5 minutes. Season with salt and pepper.

4. Pour over the macaroni, stir, and cover with the sliced cheese. Bake, uncovered, in a moderate oven at 350°F for 20 minutes, until cheese has melted. Serve immediately.

TIME: Preparation takes 15 minutes, cooking takes 40 minutes.

Spinach Lasagne

*Everyone will be asking for seconds when
they taste this delicious lasagne.*

SERVES 4

8 sheets green lasagne pasta

Spinach sauce
4 tbsps butter or margarine
3 tbsps flour
½ cup milk
1½ cups frozen spinach, thawed and
chopped finely
Pinch of ground nutmeg
Salt
Pepper

Mornay sauce
2 tbsps butter or margarine
2 tbsps flour
1 cup milk
⅓ cup Parmesan cheese, grated
1 tsp Dijon mustard
Salt

1. To make spinach sauce, heat butter in pan, stir in flour and cook gently for 30 seconds.

2. Remove from heat and stir in milk gradually. Return to heat and bring to a boil, stirring continuously. Cook for 3 minutes.

3. Add spinach, nutmeg, and salt and pepper to taste. Set aside.

4. Cook spinach lasagne in lots of boiling salted water for 10 minutes, or until tender. Rinse in cold water, and drain carefully. Dry on a clean cloth.

5. To make mornay sauce, heat butter in a saucepan and stir in flour, cooking for 30 seconds.

6. Remove from heat and stir in milk. Return to heat, stirring continuously, until boiling. Continue stirring and simmer for 3 minutes.

7. Remove from heat and add mustard and two-thirds of cheese, and salt to taste.

8. Preheat oven to 400°F. Grease an oven-proof baking dish. Line the bottom with a layer of lasagne, followed by some of the spinach mixture and a layer of the cheese sauce. Repeat the process, finishing with a layer of lasagne and a covering of cheese sauce.

9. Sprinkle with the remaining cheese. Bake in a hot oven until golden on top. Serve immediately.

Time: Preparation takes 10 minutes, cooking takes 30 minutes.

VANILLA CREAM MELBA

Elbow macaroni is enhanced with a delicious raspberry sauce and peaches in this easy-to-prepare dessert.

SERVES 4

⅔ cup small pasta or elbow macaroni
1½ cups milk
2½ tsps brown sugar
Few drops vanilla extract
½ cup heavy cream, lightly whipped
16 oz can peach halves
1 tsp cinnamon

Melba sauce
1 cup raspberries
2 tbsps confectioners sugar

1. Cook pasta in milk and sugar until soft. Stir regularly, being careful not to allow it to boil over. Remove from heat and stir in vanilla extract.

2. Pour pasta into a bowl to cool. When cool, fold in cream. Chill.

3. Meanwhile, make melba sauce. Push raspberries through a sieve, or purée in a blender or food processor. Mix in confectioners sugar to desired thickness and taste.

4. Serve pasta with peach halves and melba sauce. Dust with cinnamon if desired.

TIME: Preparation takes 15 minutes, cooking takes 10 minutes.

187

BLACK CHERRY RAVIOLI WITH SOUR CREAM SAUCE

A simple dough is mixed with cherries and cream to make the perfect ending to a meal.

SERVES 4

Dough
1¾ cups bread flour
1 tbsp sugar
3 eggs, lightly beaten

Large can pitted black cherries
¼ cup sugar
1 tsp cornstarch
½ cup sour cream
½ cup heavy cream

1. Put cherries in a sieve. Strain off the juice and reserve.

2. Make the dough by sifting flour and sugar in a bowl. Make a well in the center and add lightly-beaten eggs. Work flour and eggs together with a spoon, and then by hand, until a smooth dough is formed. Knead gently.

3. Lightly flour board, and roll dough out thinly into a rectangle. Cut dough in half. Put well-drained cherries about 1½ inches apart on the dough.

4. Place the other half on top and cut with a small glass or pastry cutter. Seal well around edges with back of a fork.

5. Boil plenty of water in a large saucepan, and drop in cherry pasta. Cook for about 10 minutes, or until they rise to the surface. Remove with a slotted spoon and keep warm. Keep 2 tablespoons cherry juice aside.

6. Mix 1 tablespoon cherry juice with cornstarch; mix remaining juice with sugar, put in small saucepan and set over heat. Add cornstarch mixture, and heat until it thickens.

7. Meanwhile mix sour cream and heavy cream together, and marble 1 tablespoon of cherry juice through it.

8. Pour hot, thickened cherry juice over cherry ravioli. Serve hot with cream sauce.

TIME: Preparation takes 30 minutes, cooking takes 15 minutes.

CHOCOLATE CREAM HELÈNE

*Pears, cream and pasta combine perfectly
in this simply delicious dessert.*

SERVES 4

⅔ cup small pasta or elbow macaroni
1½ cups milk
2½ tbsps sugar
1 tsp cocoa
½ cup heavy cream, lightly whipped
1 tbsp hot water
16 oz can pear halves

Garnish
Chocolate, grated

1. Cook pasta in milk and sugar until soft. Stir regularly, being careful not to allow it to boil over. Remove from heat.

2. Meanwhile, dissolve cocoa in hot water, and stir into pasta.

3. Pour pasta into a bowl to cool. When cool, fold in lightly-whipped cream. Chill. Serve with pear halves and a sprinkling of grated chocolate.

TIME: Preparation takes 15 minutes, cooking takes 10 minutes.

Photography by Peter Barry
Designed by Richard Hawke and Claire Leighton
Edited by Jillian Stewart and Kate Cranshaw
Recipes by Judith Ferguson, Lalita Ahmed and
   Carolyn Garner

THE
CHICKEN
COOKBOOK

® Landoll, Inc.
Ashland, Ohio 44805

Contents

CHICKEN SATAY

This typical Indonesian dish is very spicy, and makes it an excellent appetizer.

SERVES 4

2 tbsps soy sauce
2 tbsps sesame oil
2 tbsps lime juice
1 tsp ground cumin
1 tsp ground turmeric
2 tsps ground coriander
1 pound chicken breast, cut into 1-inch
    cubes
2 tbsps peanut oil
1 small onion, minced
1 tsp chili powder
½ cup crunchy peanut butter
1 tsp brown sugar
Lime wedges and coriander leaves, for
    garnish

1. Put the soy sauce, sesame oil, lime juice, cumin, turmeric, and coriander into a large bowl and mix well.

2. Add the cubed chicken to the soy sauce marinade and stir well to coat the meat evenly.

3. Cover with plastic wrap and refrigerate for at least 1 hour, but preferably overnight.

4. Drain the meat, reserving the marinade.

5. Thread the meat onto 4 large or 8 small kebob skewers and set aside.

6. Heat the peanut oil in a small saucepan and add the onion and chili powder. Cook gently until the onion is slightly softened.

7. Stir the reserved marinade into the oil-and-onion mixture, along with the peanut butter and brown sugar. Heat gently, stirring constantly, until all the ingredients are well blended.

8. If the sauce is too thick, stir in 2-4 tbsps boiling water.

9. Arrange the skewers of meat on a broiler pan and broil under moderate heat for 10-15 minutes. After the first 5 minutes of cooking, brush the skewered meat with a little of the peanut sauce to baste.

10. During the cooking time, turn the meat frequently to cook it on all sides and prevent it browning.

11. Garnish the satay with the lime and coriander leaves, and serve the remaining sauce separately.

TIME: Preparation takes about 25 minutes plus at least 1 hour marinating. Cooking takes about 15 minutes.

SERVING IDEAS: Serve with a mixed salad.

CHICKEN-STUFFED PEPPERS

This is a lighter stuffing than the usual meat-and-rice mixture.

SERVES 6

3 large green or red bell peppers
¼ butter or margarine
1 small onion, minced
1 stick celery, finely chopped
1 clove garlic, crushed
3 chicken breasts, skinned, boned, and
    diced
2 tsps chopped parsley
Salt and pepper
½ loaf of stale white bread, made into
    crumbs
1-2 eggs, beaten
6 tsps dry breadcrumbs

1. Cut the peppers in half lengthwise and remove the cores and seeds. Leave the stems attached, if wished.

2. Melt the butter in a skillet and add the onion, celery, garlic, and chicken. Cook over moderate heat until the vegetables are softened and the chicken is cooked. Add the parsley. Season with salt and pepper.

3. Stir in the stale breadcrumbs and add enough beaten egg to make the mixture hold together.

4. Spoon the filling into each pepper half, mounding the top slightly. Place the peppers in a baking dish that holds them closely together.

5. Pour enough water around the peppers to come about ½ inch up their sides. Cover, and bake in a pre-heated 350°F oven for about 45 minutes, or until the peppers are just tender.

6. Sprinkle each with the dried breadcrumbs and place under a preheated broiler. Broil until golden-brown.

TIME: Preparation takes about 30 minutes and cooking takes about 45-50 minutes.

VARIATIONS: Use green onions in place of the small onion. Add chopped nuts or black olives to the filling, if wished.

SERVING IDEAS: Serve as a first course, either hot or cold, or as a light lunch or supper with a salad.

PAOTZU STEAMED BUNS WITH CHICKEN, CABBAGE, AND MUSHROOMS

The steamed dumplings could be eaten as part of a Chinese Dim Sum meal.

MAKES about 16

3 cups self-rising flour
2 tsps salt
1 tsp fresh yeast or 1 envelope dried yeast
1 cup warm water
½ cup shredded cabbage
6 dried black Chinese mushrooms (shiitake or cloud ear) pre-soaked and sliced
2 tsps sesame oil
1 cup ground chicken
1 tbsp chopped fresh root ginger
1 tbsp soy sauce
1 tbsp oyster sauce
Black pepper

1. Place the flour and salt in a large bowl. Sprinkle the yeast over the warm water, stir and leave for 10 minutes or until foaming.

2. Make a well in the center of the flour, add the liquid and stir in well, gradually incorporating the flour. Cover with a damp cloth or plastic wrap and leave in a warm place for 2 hours or until doubled in volume.

3. Combine the shredded cabbage and mushrooms. Heat the oil in a wok and add the cabbage, mushrooms, and chicken. Stir-fry rapidly for a few minutes. Add the remaining ingredients, stir together and remove from the wok. Leave to cool.

4. Knead the dough for 2-3 minutes, then cut into about 16 pieces. Roll each piece out to a 4-inch circle and place about 2 tsps of filling in the center of each circle.

5. Draw up the edges of the dough over the filling and pinch together. Place pieces of oiled nonstick baking parchment over the pinched ends and turn the buns over so they stand on the paper.

6. Leave the buns to stand, covered with the damp cloth, for 15-20 minutes, then place in a steamer and steam rapidly for 10-15 minutes or until firm, springy, and well risen. Serve immediately.

TIME: Preparation takes about 40 minutes, plus 2 hours 20 minutes for rising. Cooking takes 10-15 minutes.

WATCHPOINT: When steaming the buns, leave enough space between them for expansion. If necessary, cook in batches.

PREPARATION: Soak the mushrooms for 20 minutes in boiling water. Discard tough stalks before using.

TACOS

Packaged taco shells make this famous Mexican snack easy to prepare, so spend the extra time on imaginative fillings.

MAKES 12

12 taco shells

Chicken Filling

3 tbsps butter or margarine
1 medium onion, chopped
1 small red bell pepper, chopped
2 tbsps flaked almonds
12 ounces chicken breasts, skinned and
    finely chopped
Salt and pepper
1 piece fresh ginger, peeled and chopped
6 tbsps milk
2 tsps cornstarch
⅔ cup sour cream

Toppings

Shredded lettuce
Grated cheese
Tomatoes, seeded and chopped
Chopped green onions
Avocado slices
Sour cream
Jalapeño peppers
Taco sauce

1. Melt 2 tbsps of the butter or margarine in a medium saucepan and add the onion. Cook slowly until softened.

2. Add the red bell pepper and almonds, and cook slowly until the almonds are lightly browned. Stir often during cooking. Remove to a plate and set aside.

3. Melt the remaining butter in the same saucepan and cook the chicken for about 5 minutes, turning frequently. Season and return the onion mixture to the pan, along with the chopped ginger.

4. Blend the milk and cornstarch and stir into the chicken mixture. Bring to the boil and stir until very thick. Mix in the sour cream and cook gently to heat through. Do not boil.

5. Heat the taco shells on a cookie sheet in a preheated 350°F oven for 2-3 minutes. Place on the sheet with the open ends downward.

6. To fill, hold the shell in one hand and spoon in about 1 tbsp of chicken filling.

7. Next, add a layer of shredded lettuce, followed by a layer of grated cheese. Add your choice of other toppings and finally spoon some taco sauce over the mixture.

TIME: Preparation takes about 30 minutes. Cooking takes about 15 minutes for the chicken filling and 2-3 minutes to heat the taco shells.

COOK'S TIP: Placing the taco shells on their open ends when reheating keeps them from closing up and makes filling easier.

SERVING IDEAS: For a buffet, place all the ingredients out separately for guests to help themselves and create their own combinations.

SZECHUAN BANG-BANG CHICKEN

Serve this dish as an appetizer. The diners should toss and mix the ingredients together themselves.

SERVES 4

2 chicken breasts
1 medium cucumber

Sauce
4 tbsps smooth peanut butter
2 tsps sesame oil
½ tsp sugar
¼ tsp salt
2 tsps broth
½ tsp chili sauce

1. Simmer the chicken in a pan of water for 30 minutes or until tender. Remove the chicken breasts and cut them into ½-inch-thick strips.

2. Thinly slice the cucumber. Spread the cucumber on a large serving platter and pile the shredded chicken on top.

3. Mix the peanut butter with the sesame oil, sugar, salt, and broth. Pour the sauce evenly over the chicken. Sprinkle the chili sauce evenly over the top.

TIME: Preparation takes about 15 minutes and cooking takes 30 minutes.

VARIATIONS: Use crunchy peanut butter or tahini in place of smooth peanut butter.

PREPARATION: The chicken is cooked if the juices run clear when a sharp knife or skewer is inserted into the thickest part of the meat.

CHICKEN SCALLOPS

There are a multitude of different methods of cooking chicken, and this one although one of the simplest, is also one of the most delicious.

SERVES 4

4 chicken breasts, boned and skinned
1 egg
8 tbsps whole-wheat breadcrumbs
1 tbsp chopped fresh sage
Salt and freshly ground black pepper
2 tbsps walnut oil
½ cup mayonnaise
⅔ cup plain yogurt
1 tsp grated fresh horseradish or daikon
2 tbsps chopped walnuts
Lemon slices and chopped walnuts to
    garnish

1. Pat the chicken breasts dry with kitchen paper.

2. Whisk the egg with a fork until it just begins to froth.

3. Carefully brush all surfaces of the chicken breasts with the egg.

4. Put the breadcrumbs onto a shallow plate and mix in the chopped sage. Season with a little salt and freshly ground black pepper.

5. Place the chicken breasts, one at a time, onto the plate, and carefully press the crumb mixture over the surfaces of the chicken.

6. Put the oil into a large shallow skillet, and gently fry the prepared chicken breasts on each side for 6-7 minutes until they are pale golden and tender. Set them aside, and keep warm.

7. Mix all the remaining ingredients except for the garnish, in a small bowl, whisking well to blend the yogurt and mayonnaise evenly.

8. Place the cooked chicken breasts on a serving dish, and spoon a little of the sauce over them. Serve garnished with the lemon slices and additional chopped nuts.

TIME: Preparation takes about 20 minutes, cooking takes about 15 minutes.

VARIATIONS: Use almonds instead of walnuts in this recipe, and limes instead of lemons. Oranges and hazelnuts make another delicious variation.

SERVING IDEAS: Serve with lightly-cooked green beans and new potatoes, or rice.

SALADE BRESSE

As well as being famous for its cheese, Bresse, in Burgundy, is renowned for its special breed of chickens, reputed to be the best in France.

SERVES 4-6

1 head radicchio, leaves separated and washed

1 head romaine lettuce, washed

1 bunch lamb's lettuce or watercress, washed

4 chicken breasts, cooked, skinned, and thinly sliced

½ cup Bresse Bleu or other blue cheese, cut in small pieces

16 cornichons (small pickles), thinly sliced

8-10 cherry tomatoes, halved and cored

2 tbsps walnut halves

Dressing

2 tbsps vegetable and walnut oil mixed

2 tsps white wine vinegar

¾ cup crème frâiche

2 tsps chopped fresh tarragon

Salt and pepper

1. Tear the radicchio and romaine lettuce into bite-size pieces. Leave the lamb's lettuce in whole leaves. If using watercress, wash thoroughly, remove the thick stems and any yellow leaves.

2. Toss the leaves together and pile onto a salad plate.

3. Place the chicken, cheese, cornichons, tomatoes, and walnuts on top of the lettuce.

4. Mix the oils and vinegar together and whisk well to emulsify.

5. Fold in the crème frâiche and add the tarragon, salt, and pepper.

6. Sprinkle some of the dressing over the salad to serve and hand the rest of the dressing separately.

TIME: Preparation takes about 20 minutes.

VARIATIONS: Use goat's cheese instead of Bresse Bleu, and yogurt or sour cream in place of the crème frâiche.

PREPARATION: The dressing can be made in advance and kept refrigerated.

CHICKEN WITH BLUEBERRY SAUCE

The sharp tang of blueberries makes an ideal partner for chicken.

SERVES 4

4 chicken breasts, boned and skinned
3 tbsps sesame oil
1 cup fresh blueberries
Juice of 1 orange
⅔ cup red wine
Sugar to taste
Orange slices and fresh blueberries to
    garnish

1. Season the chicken breasts with a little salt. Heat the oil in a skillet.

2. Gently sauté the chicken breasts for 6-7 minutes on each side, or until they are golden-brown and tender.

3. Meanwhile put the blueberries in a small pan, along with the orange juice and red wine. Bring to the boil, then cover and simmer gently until the blueberries are soft.

4. Blend the blueberries and juice using a liquidizer or food processor for 30 seconds.

5. Rub the blended purée through a fine nylon sieve, using the back of a wooden spoon, pressing the fruit through to reserve all the juice and pulp but leaving the seeds and skins in the sieve.

6. Put the sieved purée into a small saucepan and heat gently, stirring constantly until the liquid has reduced and the sauce is thick and smooth. Add a little sugar if the sauce is too sour.

7. Arrange the chicken breasts on a serving dish, and spoon the blackcurrant sauce over it. Garnish with orange slices and fresh blueberries.

TIME: Preparation takes 15 minutes, cooking takes approximately 15 minutes.

PREPARATION: To test if the chicken breasts are cooked, insert a skewer into the thickest part, then press gently. If the juices run clear, the meat is cooked.

VARIATIONS: Use cranberries instead of blueberries in this recipe.

213

PEKING EGG CHICKEN WITH BEANSPROUTS, IN ONION AND GARLIC SAUCE

This exciting mixture results in a simply delicious dish.

SERVES 3

3 chicken breasts
Salt and pepper
2 eggs
2 cloves garlic
2 green onions
4 tbsps oil
⅔ cup fresh beansprouts
4 tbsps broth
Wine vinegar to taste

1. Cut each chicken breast crosswise into 1-inch slices. Rub with salt and pepper.

2. Beat eggs lightly, and add the chicken slices to the eggs.

3. Crush the garlic and cut the green onions into 2.5cm/1-inch pieces.

4. Heat the oil in the wok. Add the chicken pieces one by one, and reduce heat to low. Leave to sauté for 2-3 minutes.

5. Once the egg has set, sprinkle the chicken with garlic, green onion, and beansprouts.

6. Finally, add the broth and vinegar to taste. Simmer gently for 4 minutes.

7. Remove the chicken, cut each piece into small regular pieces, and serve on a heated platter. Pour the remaining sauce from the wok over the chicken.

TIME: Preparation takes 10 minutes, cooking takes about 10 minutes.

COOK'S TIP: Buy the beansprouts on the day you intend to use them as they deteriorate rapidly.

SERVING IDEAS: Serve with a chili dipping sauce and rice.

CHICKEN WITH WALNUTS AND CELERY

Oyster sauce lends a subtle, slightly salty taste to this Cantonese dish.

SERVES 4

8 ounces chicken meat, cut into 1-inch
    pieces
2 tsps soy sauce
2 tsps brandy
1 tsp cornstarch
Salt and pepper
2 tbsps oil
1 clove garlic
½ cup walnut halves
3 sticks celery, cut in diagonal slices
⅔ cup chicken broth
2 tsps oyster sauce

1. Combine the chicken with the soy sauce, brandy, cornstarch, salt and pepper.

2. Heat a wok and add the oil and garlic. Cook for about 1 minute to flavor the oil.

3. Remove the garlic and add the chicken in two batches. Stir-fry quickly to cook the chicken but without allowing it to brown. Remove the chicken and add the walnuts to the wok. Cook for about 2 minutes until the walnuts are slightly brown and crisp.

4. Add the celery to the wok and cook for about 1 minute. Add the broth and oyster sauce and bring to the boil. When boiling, return the chicken to the pan and stir to coat all the ingredients well. Serve immediately.

TIME: Preparation takes about 20 minutes, cooking takes about 8 minutes.

WATCHPOINT: Nuts can burn very easily. Stir them constantly for even browning.

VARIATIONS: Almonds or cashew nuts may be used instead of the walnuts. If the cashew nuts are already roasted, add them along with the celery.

FLAUTAS

Traditionally, these are long, thin rolls of tortillas with savory fillings, topped with sour cream.

SERVES 6

8 ounces chicken, skinned, boned and ground or finely chopped
1 tbsp oil
1 small onion, minced
½ green bell pepper, finely chopped
½-1 chili, seeded and finely chopped
½ cup fresh or frozen sweetcorn
6 black olives, pitted and chopped
½ cup heavy cream
Salt
12 corn or flour tortillas
Sour cream, guacamole, and taco sauce for toppings

1. Use a food processor or meat grinder to prepare the chicken, or chop by hand.

2. Heat the oil in a medium skillet and add the chicken, onion, and green bell pepper. Cook over a moderate heat, stirring frequently to break up the pieces of chicken.

3. When the chicken is cooked and the vegetables are softened, add the chili, corn, olives, cream, and salt. Bring to the boil over a high heat and boil rapidly, stirring continuously, to reduce and thicken the cream.

4. Place 2 tortillas on a clean work surface, overlapping them by about 2 inches. Spoon some of the chicken mixture onto the tortillas, roll up and secure with cocktail sticks.

5. Fry the flautas in about ½ inch oil in a large skillet. Do not allow the tortillas to get very brown. Drain on kitchen paper.

6. Arrange flautas on serving plates and top with sour cream, guacamole, and taco sauce.

TIME: Preparation takes about 15 minutes and cooking takes about 15 minutes.

VARIATIONS: Use guacamole instead of heavy cream.

SERVING IDEAS: Flautas are often served with rice, refried beans, and a salad.

EGGPLANT AND CHICKEN CHILI

This unusual dish is both delicious and filling.

SERVES 4

---

2 medium-sized eggplants
4 tbsps sesame oil
2 cloves garlic, crushed
4 green onions thinly sliced, diagonally
1 green chili, finely chopped
12 ounces boned and skinned chicken breast
4 tbsps light soy sauce
2 tbsps broth, or water
1 tbsp tomato paste
1 tsp cornstarch
Sugar to taste

---

1. Cut the eggplants into quarters lengthwise, using a sharp knife. Slice the eggplant quarters into pieces approximately ½-inch thick.

2. Put the eggplant slices into a bowl and sprinkle liberally with salt. Stir well to coat evenly. Cover with plastic wrap and leave to stand for 30 minutes.

3. Rinse the eggplant slices very thoroughly under running water, then pat dry.

4. Heat half of the oil in a wok, or large skillet, and gently cook the garlic until it is soft, but not colored.

5. Add the eggplant slices to the wok and cook, stirring frequently, for 3-4 minutes.

6. Stir the green onions together with the chili into the cooked eggplant, and cook for a further 1 minute. Remove from the pan, and set aside, keeping warm.

7. Cut the chicken breast into thin slices with a sharp knife.

8. Heat the remaining 2 tbsps of oil in the wok, and fry the chicken slices for approximately 2 minutes, or until they have turned white and are thoroughly cooked.

9. Return the eggplant and green onions to the pan and cook, stirring continuously, for 2 minutes or until heated through completely.

10. Mix together the remaining ingredients and pour these over the chicken and eggplants in the wok, stirring constantly until the sauce has thickened and cleared. Serve immediately.

TIME: Preparation takes about 10 minutes plus 30 minutes marinating, cooking takes approximately 15 minutes.

COOK'S TIP: The vegetables can be prepared well in advance, but the eggplants should be removed from the salt after 30 minutes, or they will become too dehydrated.

VARIATIONS: Use zucchini in place of the eggplants if wished.

CHICKEN WITH CLOUD EARS

Cloud ears is the delightful name for an edible tree fungus which is mushroom-like in taste and texture.

SERVES 6

12 cloud ears, wood ears, or other dried Chinese mushrooms, soaked in boiling water for 5 minutes
1 pound chicken breasts, boned and thinly sliced crosswise
1 egg white
2 tsps cornstarch
2 tsps white wine
2 tsps sesame oil
1¼ cups oil
1-inch piece fresh root ginger
1 clove garlic
1¼ cups chicken broth
1 tbsp cornstarch
3 tbsps light soy sauce
Pinch salt and pepper

1. Soak the mushrooms until they soften and swell. Remove all the skin and bone from the chicken and cut it into thin slices. Mix the chicken with the egg white, cornstarch, wine, and sesame oil.

2. Heat the wok for a few minutes and add the oil. Add the whole piece of ginger and whole garlic clove to the oil and cook about 1 minute. Remove them and reduce the heat.

3. Add about a quarter of the chicken at a time and stir-fry for about 1 minute. Remove, and continue cooking until all the chicken is fried. Remove all but about 2 tbsps of the oil from the wok.

4. Drain the mushrooms and squeeze them to extract all the liquid. If using mushrooms with stems, remove the stems before slicing the caps thinly. Cut cloud ears or wood ears into smaller pieces. Add to the wok and cook for about 1 minute.

5. Add the broth and allow it to come almost to the boil. Mix together the cornstarch and soy sauce and add a tablespoon of the hot broth. Add the mixture to the wok, stirring constantly, and bring to the boil. Allow to boil for 1-2 minutes or until thickened. The sauce will clear when the cornstarch has cooked sufficiently.

6. Return the chicken to the wok and add salt and pepper. Stir thoroughly for about 1 minute and serve immediately.

TIME: Preparation takes about 25 minutes, cooking takes about 5 minutes.

VARIATIONS: Flat, cup, or button mushrooms may be used instead of the dried mushrooms. Eliminate the soaking and slice them thickly. Cook as for the dried variety. Two tsps bottled oyster sauce may be added with the broth.

SERVING SUGGESTION: Cloud ears or wood ears are both available from oriental supermarkets and some delicatessens. Shiitake mushrooms are more readily available fresh or dried. Both keep a long time in their dried state.

CHICKEN, HAM, AND LEEK PIE

The addition of cream and egg yolks at the end of the cooking time makes this pie extra special.

SERVES 6-8

---

1 × 3-pound chicken
1 onion
1 bayleaf
Parsley stalks
Salt and black pepper
1 pound leeks
2 tbsps butter
½ cup chopped cooked ham
1 tbsp parsley
1¼ cups chicken broth
12-14 ounces puff dough
⅔ cup heavy cream
1 egg, lightly beaten for glazing

---

1. Put the cleaned chicken in a large saucepan together with the onion, bayleaf, parsley stalks, and salt and pepper. Cover with cold water and bring gently to the boil. Allow to simmer for about 45 minutes until the chicken is tender. Leave it to cool in the pan.

2. Meanwhile, wash and trim the leeks, and cut into 1½-inch pieces. Melt the butter in a small pan and gently sauté the leeks for about 5 minutes. Remove from the heat.

3. Take the cooled chicken out of the pan, remove the skin, and strip off the flesh. Cut it into good-sized pieces.

4. Put the chicken, ham, leeks, and parsley into a large pie dish with plenty of seasoning. Add 1¼ cups of the cooking liquid from the chicken.

5. Roll out the dough slightly larger than the size of the pie dish. Use the trimmings to line the rim of the dish. Dampen them and put on the dough lid. Trim and seal the edges together firmly. Any surplus dough can be used to make decorative leaves. Cut a few slits in the dough to allow the steam to escape. Brush the dough well with beaten egg.

6. Bake in the center of a preheated 450°F oven for 15 minutes. Remove and glaze again with beaten egg. Reduce the temperature of the oven to 400°F. Return the pie to the oven for another 20 minutes.

7. When the pie crust is well risen and golden-brown, remove it from the oven. Carefully lift off a segment of pastry and pour in the cream which has been gently warmed together with the remaining beaten egg.

TIME: Preparation takes about 45 minutes for the chicken, plus extra cooling time and 20 minutes to prepare the pie. Cooking takes about 35 minutes.

SERVING IDEAS: Serve with creamed potatoes and a green vegetable.

CRUMB-FRIED CHICKEN

A southern speciality, this dish has a slightly misleading name since most of the "frying" takes place in the oven!

SERVES 4-6

---

1 ✖ 3-pound chicken
1 cup dry breadcrumbs
½ cup Parmesan cheese
¼ tsp ground ginger
2 eggs, mixed with a pinch of salt
3 tbsps oil
¼ cup butter or margarine
Lemons and parsley for garnish

---

1. Preheat the oven to 400°F. To joint the chicken, first cut off the legs, bending them outward to break the ball-and-socket joint. Cut in between the ball-and-socket joint to completely remove the legs.

2. Cut down the breastbone with sharp poultry shears to separate the two halves. Use the poultry shears to cut through the rib cage. Use the notch in the shears to separate the wing joints from the back.

3. Use a sharp knife to separate the drumstick from the thigh. Cut the breasts in half with poultry shears.

4. Mix the breadcrumbs, Parmesan cheese, and ground ginger together. First dip the chicken into the egg and then coat with the crumbs.

5. Heat the oil in a large skillet and add the butter. When hot, place in the chicken, skin side down first. Cook both sides until golden-brown.

6. Transfer with a slotted spoon to a cookie sheet and place in the oven for 20-30 minutes, or until the juices run clear when the chicken is tested with a knife or a fork. Serve garnished with small bunches of parsley and lemon wedges or slices.

TIME: Preparation takes about 30 minutes. If using chicken portions, allow about 15-20 minutes for preparation. Chicken will take about 10-15 minutes to brown and 20-30 minutes to finish cooking in the oven.

PREPARATION: Mix the crumbs, cheese, and ginger on a sheet of wax or parchment paper. Place the chicken on the crumbs and shake the paper from side to side to coat easily and completely.

VARIATIONS: If wished, omit the Parmesan cheese and ginger, and add extra breadcrumbs, paprika, salt, pepper, and a pinch of thyme.

INDIAN CHICKEN

Marinating chicken with spices allows their full flavors to penetrate the meat.

SERVES 4-6

---

1 × 3-pound chicken, cut into 8 pieces

2½ cups plain yogurt

2 tsps ground coriander

2 tsps paprika

1 tsp ground turmeric

Juice of 1 lime

1 tbsp honey

½ clove garlic, crushed

1 small piece ginger, peeled and grated

---

1. Pierce the chicken all over with a fork or skewer.

2. Combine all the remaining ingredients and spread half the mixture over the chicken, rubbing in well.

3. Place the chicken in a shallow dish or a plastic bag and cover or tie it. Leave for at least 4 hours or overnight in the refrigerator.

4. Arrange the chicken, skin side down, under a moderate pre-heated broiler and cook until lightly browned. Turn over and cook the second side until lightly browned. This should take about 30 minutes in all. Baste frequently with remaining marinade.

5. Reduce the broiler heat and cook for 15 minutes, turning and basting frequently, until the chicken is brown and the skin is crisp.

6. Alternatively, bake the chicken in a covered pan in the oven at 325°F for 45 minutes - 1 hour and broil it for the last 15 minutes for flavor and color.

7. Serve any remaining yogurt mixture separately as a sauce.

TIME: Preparation takes about 15 minutes and marinating at least 4 hours, cooking takes about 45 minutes.

COOK'S TIP: The chicken can also be barbecued. Make sure the shelf is on the level furthest from the coals so that the chicken has time to cook without burning.

VARIATIONS: Use chicken breasts only for this dish.

CHICKEN AND VEGETABLE STEW

A combination of chicken, lima beans, peppers, and onions made into an aromatic stew.

SERVES 4-6

1 × 3-pound chicken, cut in 8 pieces
⅓ cup butter or margarine
3 tbsps flour
1 large red bell pepper, diced
1 large green bell pepper, diced
6 green onions, chopped
2 cups chicken broth
⅔ cup canned or fresh lima beans
1 tsp chopped thyme
Salt, pepper, and a pinch of nutmeg

1. To cut the chicken in 8 pieces, remove the legs first. Cut between the legs and the body of the chicken.

2. Bend the legs outward to break the joint and cut away from the body.

3. Cut the drumstick and thigh joints in half.

4. Cut down the breastbone with a sharp knife, and then use poultry shears to cut through the bone and ribcage to remove the breast joints from the back.

5. Cut both breast joints in half, leaving some white meat attached to the wing joint.

6. Heat the butter in a large skillet and when foaming add the chicken, skin side down. Brown on one side, turn over and brown the other side. Remove the chicken and add the flour to the pan. Cook to a pale straw color. Add the peppers and onions and cook briefly.

7. Gradually stir in the chicken broth and bring to the boil. Stir constantly until thickened. Add the chicken, lima beans, thyme, seasoning, and nutmeg. Cover the pan and cook about 25 minutes, or until the chicken is tender.

TIME: Preparation takes about 35 minutes and cooking takes about 40 minutes.

PREPARATION: For crisper vegetables, add them after the chicken and sauce have cooked for about 15 minutes.

SERVING SUGGESTION: Buying a whole chicken and jointing it yourself is cheaper than buying chicken joints.

CHICKEN WITH SAFFRON RICE AND PEAS

Saffron is frequently used in Spanish recipes. While it is expensive, it gives rice and sauces a lovely golden color and delicate flavor.

SERVES 4

2 tbsps oil
1 × 2-3 pound chicken, cut into 8 pieces, skinned if wished
Salt and pepper
1 small onion, minced
2 tsps paprika
1 clove garlic, crushed
8 tomatoes, skinned, seeded, and chopped
1¼ cups rice
3 cups boiling water
Large pinch saffron or ¼ tsp ground saffron
¾ cup frozen peas
2 tbsps chopped parsley

1. Heat the oil in a large skillet. Season the chicken with salt and pepper and place it in the hot oil, skin side down first. Cook over moderate heat, turning the chicken frequently to brown it lightly. Set the chicken aside.

2. Add the onions to the oil and cook slowly until softened but not colored.

3. Add the paprika and cook for about 2 minutes, stirring frequently until the paprika loses some of its red color. Add the garlic and the tomatoes.

4. Cook the mixture over high heat for about 5 minutes to evaporate the liquid from the tomatoes. The mixture should be of dropping consistency when done. Add the rice, water, and saffron and stir together.

5. Return the chicken to the casserole and bring to the boil over high heat. Reduce to simmering, cover tightly, and cook for about 20 minutes. Remove chicken and add the peas and parsley. Cook a further 5-10 minutes, or until rice is tender. Combine with the chicken to serve.

TIME: Preparation takes about 20-25 minutes and cooking takes about 25-35 minutes.

VARIATIONS: Use fresh peas, podded, in which case allow about 3 cups of peas in their pods. Cook fresh peas with the rice and chicken.

SERVING IDEAS: This is a very casual, peasant-type dish which is traditionally served in the casserole in which it was cooked.

CHICKEN COBBLER

This dish is warming winter fare with its creamy sauce and tender, light topping.

SERVES 6

4 chicken joints (2 breasts and 2 legs)
1½ quarts water
1 bayleaf
4 whole peppercorns
2 carrots, peeled and diced
24 pearl onions, peeled
6 tbsps frozen sweetcorn
⅔ cup heavy cream
Salt

Cobbler Topping

3½ cups all-purpose flour
1½ tbsps double-action baking powder
Pinch salt
5 tbsps butter or margarine
1½ cups milk
1 egg, beaten with a pinch of salt

1. Place the chicken in a deep saucepan with the water, bayleaf, and peppercorns. Cover and bring to the boil. Reduce the heat and allow to simmer for 20-30 minutes, or until the chicken is tender. Remove the chicken from the pan and allow to cool. Skim and discard the fat from the surface of the cooking liquid.

2. Continue to simmer the broth until reduced by about half. Meanwhile, skin the chicken and remove the meat from the bones. Strain the broth and add the carrots and onions. Cook until tender and add the corn. Stir in the cream, season and add the chicken. Pour into a warmed casserole or into individual baking dishes and keep hot.

3. To prepare the topping, sift the dry ingredients into a bowl or place them in a food processor and process once or twice to sift.

4. Rub in the butter or margarine until the mixture resembles breadcrumbs. Stir in enough of the milk to allow the mixture to stick together. If using a food processor, trickle the milk in down the food tube and process in short bursts to avoid overmixing.

5. Turn out onto a floured surface and knead lightly. Roll out with a floured rolling pin until the dough is about ½-inch thick.

6. Cut the dough into rounds using a 2-inch cookie cutter to form the cobbles. Place the rounds on top of the chicken mixture. Brush the surface of the cobbler with the egg and salt mixture and bake for 10-15 minutes in a pre-heated oven at 375°F. Serve immediately.

TIME: Preparation takes about 20-30 minutes for the chicken, about 20 minutes to prepare the sauce, and the cobbler takes about 10 minutes to prepare. Final cooking takes about 10-15 minutes.

PREPARATION: Once the topping has been prepared, it must be baked immediately or the baking powder will stop working and the cobbler topping will not rise.

LEMON CHICKEN

Chicken, lemon, and basil is an ideal flavor combination and one that is used often in Greek cookery.

SERVES 4-6

---

2 tbsps olive oil
2 tbsps butter or margarine
1 × 3-pound chicken, jointed
1 small onion, cut in thin strips
2 sticks celery, shredded
2 carrots, cut in julienne strips
1 tbsp chopped fresh basil
1 bayleaf
Grated rind and juice of 2 small lemons
⅔ cup water
Salt and pepper
Pinch sugar (optional)
Lemon slices for garnishing

---

1. Heat the oil in a large skillet. Add the butter or margarine and, when foaming, add the chicken, skin side down, in one layer. Brown and turn over. Brown the other side. Cook the chicken in two batches if necessary. Remove the chicken to a plate and set aside.

2. Add the vegetables and cook for 2-3 minutes over a moderate heat. Add the basil, bayleaf, lemon rind, and juice, water, salt, and pepper and replace the chicken. Bring the mixture to the boil.

3. Cover the pan and reduce the heat. Allow to simmer about 35-45 minutes or until the chicken is tender and the juices run clear when the thighs are pierced with a fork.

4. Remove the chicken and vegetables to a serving dish and discard the bayleaf. The sauce should be thick, so boil to reduce if necessary. If the sauce is too tart, add a pinch of sugar. Spoon the sauce over the chicken to serve and garnish with the lemon slices.

TIME: Preparation takes about 30 minutes, cooking takes about 45-55 minutes total, including browning of chicken.

VARIATIONS: Use limes instead of lemons and oregano instead of basil.

SERVING IDEAS: In Greece, this dish is often served with pasta. Rice is also a good accompaniment, along with a green salad.

TOMATO AND BACON FRIED CHICKEN

This unusual version of fried chicken is cooked in a tomato sauce flavored with garlic, herbs, and wine.

SERVES 6

Flour for dredging
Salt and pepper
1 × 3-pound chicken, cut into portions
6 tbsps oil
5 tbsps butter or margarine
1 clove garlic, crushed
1 small onion, finely chopped
½ cup diced bacon
6 tomatoes, skinned and chopped
2 tsps fresh thyme or 1 tsp dried thyme
Salt and pepper
⅔ cup white wine
2 tbsps chopped parsley

1. Mix the flour with salt and pepper and dredge the chicken lightly, shaking the pieces to remove any excess. Heat the oil in a large skillet and, when hot, add the butter.

2. Add the chicken drumstick and thigh pieces, skin side down, and allow to brown. Turn the pieces over and brown on the other side. Brown over moderately low heat so that the chicken cooks as well as browns. Push the chicken to one side of the pan, add the breast meat, and brown in the same way.

3. Add the garlic, onion, and bacon to the pan and reduce the heat. Cook slowly for about 10 minutes, or until the bacon browns slightly. Add the tomatoes and thyme, and reduce the heat. Cook until the chicken is just tender and the tomatoes are softened.

4. Using a slotted spoon, transfer the chicken and other ingredients to a serving dish and keep warm. Remove all but about 4 tbsps of the fat from the pan and deglaze with the wine, scraping up the browned bits from the bottom. Bring to the boil and allow to reduce slightly. Pour this gravy over the chicken to serve, and sprinkle with chopped parsley.

TIME: Preparation takes about 25 minutes and cooking takes about 30-40 minutes.

PREPARATION: Brown the chicken slowly so that it cooks at the same time as it browns. This will cut down on the length of cooking time needed once all the ingredients are added.

SPICY SPANISH CHICKEN

*Chili, coriander, and bright red tomatoes add a warm Spanish flavor
to broiled chicken.*

SERVES 6

---

6 boned chicken breasts

Grated rind and juice of 1 lime

2 tbsps olive oil

Coarsely ground black pepper

6 tbsps whole-grain mustard

2 tsps paprika

4 ripe tomatoes, skinned, de-seeded, and
    quartered

2 shallots, chopped

1 clove garlic, crushed

½ jalapeño pepper or other chili, seeded
    and chopped

1 tsp wine vinegar

Pinch salt

2 tbsps chopped fresh coriander

Whole coriander leaves to garnish

---

1. Place the chicken breasts in a shallow dish with the lime rind and juice, oil, pepper, mustard, and paprika. Marinate for about 1 hour, turning occasionally.

2. To skin the tomatoes easily, drop them into boiling water for about 5 seconds or less, depending on ripeness. Place immediately in cold water. Skins should come off easily.

3. Place the tomatoes, shallots, garlic, chili, vinegar, and salt in a food processor or blender, and process until coarsely chopped. Stir in the coriander by hand.

4. Place the chicken on a broiler pan and reserve the marinade. Cook the chicken, skin side uppermost, for about 7-10 minutes, depending on how close it is to the heat source. Baste frequently with the remaining marinade. Broil the other side in the same way. Sprinkle with salt after broiling.

5. Place the chicken on serving dishes and garnish the top with coriander leaves or sprigs. Serve with a spoonful of the tomato relish on one side.

TIME: Preparation takes about 1 hour including marinating, and cooking
takes 14-20 minutes.

PREPARATION: The tomato relish can be prepared in advance and kept in
the refrigerator.

WATCHPOINT: When preparing chilies, wear rubber gloves or at least be
sure to wash hands thoroughly after handling them. Do not touch eyes or
face before washing hands.

CHICKEN POLISH STYLE

Choose small, young chickens for a truly Polish-style dish. A dry white roll was originally used for stuffing, but breadcrumbs are easier.

SERVES 4

2 × 2-pound chickens
1 tbsp butter or margarine
2 chicken livers
6 slices crustless bread, made into crumbs
2 tsps minced parsley
1 tsp chopped dill
1 egg
Salt and pepper
⅔ cup chicken broth

1. Remove the fat from just inside the cavities of the chickens and discard it. Melt the butter in a small skillet. Pick over the chicken livers and cut away any discolored parts. Add chicken livers to the butter and cook until just brown. Chop and set aside.

2. Combine the breadcrumbs, herbs, egg, salt, and pepper and mix well. Mix in the chopped chicken livers.

3. Stuff the cavities of the chickens and sew up the openings. Tie the legs together.

4. Place the chickens in a roasting pan and spread the breasts and legs lightly with more butter. Pour the broth around the chickens and roast in a preheated 375°F oven for about 40-45 minutes. Baste frequently with the pan juices during roasting.

5. To check if the chickens are done, pierce the thickest part of the thigh with a skewer or small, sharp knife. If the juices run clear the chickens are ready. If the juices are pink, return to the oven for another 5-10 minutes.

6. When the chickens are done, remove them from the roasting pan, remove the string, and keep them warm. Skim any fat from the surface of the pan juices. If a lot of liquid has accumulated, pour into a small saucepan and reduce over high heat. Pour the juices over the chicken to serve.

TIME: Preparation takes about 20 minutes and cooking takes about 45 minutes.

SERVING IDEAS: Serve with a cucumber salad or a Polish style lettuce salad and new potatoes tossed with butter and dill.

VARIATIONS: Chopped mushrooms or onions may be added to the stuffing, if wished.

CHICKEN, SAUSAGE, AND OKRA STEW

There is an exotic flavor to this economical chicken stew. The garlic sausage adds flavor instantly.

SERVES 4-6

½ cup oil
1 × 3-pound chicken, cut into 6-8 pieces
1 cup flour
1 large onion, minced
1 large green bell pepper, roughly chopped
3 sticks celery, finely chopped
2 cloves garlic, crushed
8 ounces garlic sausage, diced
5 cups chicken broth
1 bayleaf
Dash Tabasco
Salt and pepper
1 cup fresh okra
Cooked rice to serve

1. Heat the oil in a large skillet and brown the chicken all over, 3-4 pieces at a time. Transfer the chicken to a plate and set it aside.

2. Reduce the heat under the pan and add the flour. Cook over a very low heat for about 30 minutes, stirring constantly until the flour turns a rich, dark brown. Take the pan off the heat occasionally, so that the flour does not burn.

3. Add the onion, green bell pepper, celery, garlic, and sausage to the pan and cook for about 5 minutes over very low heat, stirring continuously.

4. Slowly add the broth, stirring constantly, and bring to the boil. Add the bayleaf, a dash of Tabasco and seasoning. Return the chicken to the pan, cover and cook for about 30 minutes or until the chicken is tender.

5. Top and tail the okra and cut each into 2-3 pieces. If the okra are small, leave whole. Add to the chicken and cook for a further 10-15 minutes. Remove the bayleaf and serve over rice.

TIME: Preparation takes about 30 minutes and cooking takes about 1 hour 25 minutes.

COOK'S TIP: The oil-and-flour paste may be made ahead of time and kept in the refrigerator to use whenever needed. If the paste is cold, heat the liquid before adding.

FRIED CHICKEN

Fried Chicken is easy to make at home and it's much tastier than a takeout!

SERVES 4

2 eggs
3 pounds chicken portions
2 cups flour
1 tsp each salt, paprika, and sage
½ tsp black pepper
Pinch cayenne pepper (optional)
Oil for frying
Parsley or watercress to garnish

1. Beat the eggs in a large bowl and add the chicken one piece at a time, turning to coat.

2. Mix flour and seasonings in a large plastic bag.

3. Place the chicken in the bag one piece at a time, close bag tightly, and shake to coat. Alternatively, dip each chicken piece in a bowl of seasoned flour, shaking off the excess.

4. Heat about ½ inch of oil in a large skillet.

5. When the oil is hot, add the chicken, skin side downward first. Fry for about 12 minutes and then turn over. Fry a further 12 minutes or until the juices run clear.

6. Drain the chicken on kitchen paper and serve immediately. Garnish with parsley or watercress.

TIME: Preparation takes about 20 minutes and cooking takes about 24 minutes.

PREPARATION: The chicken should not be crowded in the skillet. If the pan is small, fry the chicken in several batches.

COOK'S TIP: When coating food for frying, be sure to coat it just before cooking. If left to stand, the coating can become soggy.

Tangerine Peel Chicken

An exotic mixture of flavors blends perfectly in this delicious chicken dish.

SERVES 2

1 pound boned chicken breast, cut into
 1-inch pieces

Seasoning

½ tsp salt

1½ tsps sugar

½ tsp monosodium glutamate (optional)

1 tsp dark soy sauce

2 tsps light soy sauce

1 tsp rice wine or dry sherry

2 tsps vinegar

1 tsp sesame oil

2 tsps cornstarch

Oil for deep frying

1-2 red or green chilies, chopped

½-inch fresh root ginger, peeled and finely
 chopped

2 inches dried tangerine peel, coarsely
 ground or crumbled

2 green onions, finely chopped

Sauce

½ tsp cornstarch

1-2 tbsps water or broth

1. Mix the chicken pieces with the seasoning ingredients and stir well. Leave to marinate for 10-15 minutes. Remove the chicken pieces and reserve the marinade.

2. Heat a wok and add the oil for deep frying. Heat to 350°F, add the chicken pieces, and fry for 4-5 minutes until golden. Drain chicken on kitchen paper and keep hot.

3. Allow the oil to cool then pour off, leaving 1 tbsp oil in the wok. Stir-fry the chilies, ginger, tangerine peel, and green onions for 2-3 minutes. When they begin to turn color add the chicken and stir-fry for 1 minute.

4. Mix the reserved marinade with the sauce ingredients and pour this over the chicken. Stir and cook for 2-3 minutes until the sauce thickens and the chicken is tender. Serve immediately.

TIME: Preparation takes 20 minutes including marinating time, cooking takes 15-20 minutes.

PREPARATION: Cook the chicken in batches.

COOK'S TIP: Have all the ingredients ready prepared before starting to cook.

CHICKEN WITH BEANSPROUTS

Marinated chicken, is stir-fried with beansprouts and served with a sauce based on the marinade.

SERVES 4

4 boneless chicken breasts, skinned
1 tbsp Chinese rice wine
2 tsps cornstarch
½ cup beansprouts
2 tbsps oil
2 green onions, finely sliced
1 tsp sugar
1¼ cups chicken broth
Salt and pepper

1. Cut the chicken into thin slices or strips.

2. Place the chicken on a plate and pour the Chinese rice wine over it.

3. Sprinkle with the cornstarch and stir together well. Leave to marinate for 30 minutes.

4. Blanch the beansprouts in boiling, lightly-salted water for 1 minute. Rinse under cold running water and set aside to drain.

5. Remove the chicken from the marinade with a slotted spoon. Heat the oil in a wok and stir-fry the green onions and the chicken for 2-3 minutes.

6. Add the drained beansprouts and the sugar. Add the marinade and the broth. Allow to heat through. Check the seasoning, adding salt and pepper to taste. Serve immediately.

TIME: Preparation takes about 20 minutes, marinating takes 30 minutes and cooking takes approximately 8-10 minutes.

VARIATIONS: Use half a small ordinary onion if green onions are not available.

WATCHPOINT: As soon as you add the marinade to the wok, the mixture will thicken so have the stock ready to pour in immediately and stir continuously until all the ingredients have been fully incorporated.

CHICKEN AND SAUSAGE RISOTTO

This is a one-pot meal you can cook on the stove top.

SERVES 4-6

---

3 pounds chicken portions, skinned, boned, and cut into cubes
3 tbsps butter or margarine
1 large onion, coarsely chopped
3 sticks celery, coarsely chopped
1 large green bell pepper, coarsely chopped
1 clove garlic, crushed
Salt and pepper
1 cup uncooked rice
1 × 14-ounce can tomatoes
6 ounces smoked sausage, cut into ½-inch dice
4 cups chicken broth
Minced parsley

1. Use the chicken skin and bones and the onion and celery trimmings to make the broth. Cover the ingredients with water, bring to the boil and then simmer slowly for 1 hour. Strain and reserve.

2. Melt the butter or margarine in a large saucepan and add the onion. Cook slowly to brown and then add the celery, green pepper, and garlic and cook briefly.

3. Add the salt and pepper and the rice, stirring to mix well.

4. Add the chicken, tomatoes, sausage, and broth and mix well. Bring to the boil, then reduce the heat to simmering and cook for about 20-25 minutes, stirring occasionally, until the chicken is done and the rice is tender. The rice should have absorbed most of the liquid by the time it has cooked. Sprinkle with the minced parsley to serve.

TIME: Preparation takes about 1 hour and cooking takes about 30-35 minutes.

PREPARATION: Check the level of liquid occasionally as the rice is cooking and add more water or broth as necessary. If there is a lot of liquid left and the rice is nearly cooked, uncover the pan and boil rapidly.

SERVING IDEAS: Add a green salad to make a complete meal.

CHICKEN IN HOT PEPPER SAUCE

Stir-fried chicken served with peppers in a hot sauce.

SERVES 4

4 boned chicken breasts, skinned
2 tbsps oil
1 tsp chopped garlic
1 green bell pepper, cut into thin strips
1 red bell pepper, cut into thin strips
1 tsp wine vinegar
1 tbsp light soy sauce
1 tsp sugar
1½ cups chicken broth
1 tbsp chili sauce
2 tsps cornstarch
Salt and pepper

1. Cut the chicken breasts crosswise into thin strips.

2. Heat the oil in a wok and stir-fry the garlic, chicken, and the green and red bell peppers for 3-4 minutes.

3. Pour off any excess oil and deglaze the wok with the vinegar. Stir in the soy sauce, sugar, and broth.

4. Gradually stir in the chili sauce, tasting after each addition. Season with a little salt and pepper to taste.

5. Blend the cornstarch with a little water and stir into the wok. Bring to the boil then simmer for 2-3 minutes. Serve piping hot.

TIME: Preparation takes 10 minutes and cooking takes approximately 10 minutes.

COOK'S TIP: Have all your ingredients ready prepared and measured out before you start to cook.

SERVING IDEAS: Serve with boiled or egg fried rice, on its own or as part of a Chinese meal.

CHICKEN IN SWEET-AND-SOUR SAUCE

This is an Italian agrodolce recipe more unusual than the familiar Chinese sweet-and-sauce flavours.

SERVES 4–6

2½ pounds chicken joints
1 large onion, chopped
1 large carrot, chopped
5 tbsps maraschino
5 tbsps white wine vinegar
140ml/¼ pint water
1 bayleaf
15 juniper berries
4 tbsps olive oil
Salt and pepper

1. Marinate the chicken joints for 4–6 hours in the chopped onion, carrot, liqueur, vinegar, water, juniper berries, and bayleaf.

2. Take the joints from the marinade and drain well, reserving the marinade. Sauté the joints in the olive oil until golden.

3. Place the joints in a shallow casserole, add the unstrained marinade, cover and cook at 350°F for a about 1 hour or until the chicken is tender. Place on a warmed serving platter and keep warm.

4. Remove the bayleaf and press the cooking juices through a sieve. Reheat gently and pour the juices over the chicken to serve.

TIME: Allow 4–6 hours for the chicken to marinate. Cooking takes about 1 hour.

SERVING IDEAS: Accompany with pasta and an Italian bread such as Ciabatta.

CHICKEN WITH RED PEPPERS

Easy as this recipe is, it looks and tastes good enough for company.

SERVES 4

4 large red bell peppers
4 skinned and boned chicken breasts
1½ tbsps oil
Salt and pepper
1 clove garlic, finely chopped
3 tbsps white wine vinegar
2 green onions, finely chopped
Sage leaves for garnish

1. Cut the peppers in half and remove the stems, cores, and seeds. Flatten the peppers with the palm of your hand and brush the skin sides lightly with oil.

2. Place the peppers skin side upward on the rack of a preheated broiler and cook about 2 inches away from the heat source until the skins are well blistered and charred.

3. Seal the peppers in a thick plastic bag and allow them to stand until cool. Peel off the skins with a small vegetable knife. Cut peppers into thin strips and set aside.

4. Place the chicken breasts between two sheets of dampened parchment paper and flatten by hitting with a rolling pin or steak hammer.

5. Heat the oil in a large skillet. Season the chicken breasts on both sides and add to the pan. Cook 5 minutes, turn over and cook until tender, lightly browned, and cooked through. Remove the chicken and keep it warm.

6. Add the pepper strips, garlic, vinegar, and green onions to the pan and cook briefly until the vinegar loses its strong aroma.

7. Place the chicken breasts on serving plates. Spoon the pan juices over them.

8. Arrange the pepper mixture over the chicken and garnish with the sage leaves.

TIME: Preparation takes about 35-40 minutes and cooking takes about 10 minutes to char the peppers and about 15 minutes to finish the dish.

VARIATIONS: For convenience, the dish may be prepared with canned pimento instead of red bell peppers. These will be softer so cook the garlic, vinegar and onions to soften, and then add pimento.

SERVING SUGGESTION: If fresh sage is unavailable substitute coriander or parsley leaves as a garnish.

259

CHICKEN AND PANCETTA ROLLS

These rolls can be prepared in advance and kept chilled until cooking time. They make perfect dinner party fare.

SERVES 4

---

4 large chicken breasts, skinned
⅓ cup butter, softened
1 clove garlic, crushed
1 tbsp fresh oregano leaves or 1 tsp dried oregano
Salt and pepper
16 slices pancetta or prosciutto ham
Oil

---

1. Place each chicken breast between two sheets of damp parchment paper and beat out each piece with a rolling pin or steak hammer to flatten.

2. Mix the butter, garlic, oregano, salt, and pepper together. Spread half of the mixture over each chicken scallop, then lay 4 slices of pancetta on top of each. Roll up, tucking in the sides, and secure with cocktail sticks. Spread the remaining butter on the outside of each roll.

3. Cook the rolls under a medium hot preheated broiler for about 15-20 minutes, turning occasionally, until tender. Slice each roll into ½-inch rounds to serve.

TIME: Preparation takes about 20 minutes and cooking takes 15-20 minutes.

VARIATIONS: The chicken rolls can be sautéed in a skillet.

SERVING IDEAS: Serve with a fresh tomato sauce, and accompany with rice or new potatoes, and green beans.

BLUE CHEESE CHICKEN

These chicken parcels make a lovely and unusual dish for a dinner party.

SERVES 4

---

4 ounces blue cheese

⅔ cup butter

2 tbsps heavy cream

1 tbsp parsley, finely chopped

4 chicken breasts, skinned, boned, and beaten flat

8 slices bacon

2 tbsps oil

2 tbsps butter

⅔ cup dry white wine

⅔ cup chicken broth

Salt and pepper

2 tsps cornstarch

---

1. In a bowl, cream together the cheese and butter then add the cream to make a spreading consistency. Add the parsley.

2. Spread the cheese mixture on one side only of the chicken breasts, leaving a narrow border. Roll the breasts up, wrap each one in 2 bacon rashers and secure with a cocktail stick or skewer.

3. In a flameproof casserole, heat the oil and butter together and, when sizzling, brown the chicken parcels on each side until golden.

4. Pour in the wine, chicken broth and seasoning (use very little salt because the cheese stuffing will be quite salty). Bring to the boil, cover, and simmer gently for about 40 minutes, turning occasionally.

5. When cooked, transfer the chicken to a hot serving dish and remove the sticks or skewers.

6. Blend the cornstarch in a cup with a little cold water and add to the pan juices. Stir until the sauce thickens, adjust seasoning if necessary, and pour the gravy over the chicken. Serve at once.

TIME: Preparation takes about 25 minutes and cooking takes 45-50 minutes.

PREPARATION: The chicken parcels can be prepared in advance of cooking and refrigerated until required.

SERVING IDEAS: Serve with rice or new potatoes and broccoli.

CHICKEN WITH OLIVES

*This is a chicken sauté dish for olive-lovers. Use more or less of them
as your own taste dictates.*

SERVES 4-6

2 tbsps olive oil
2 tbsps butter or margarine
3 pounds chicken portions
1 clove garlic, crushed
⅔ cup white wine
⅔ cup chicken broth
Salt and pepper
4 zucchini, cut in ½-inch pieces
20 pitted black and green olives
2 tbsps minced parsley

1. Heat the oil in a large skillet and add the butter or margarine. When foaming, add the chicken, skin side down, in one layer. Brown one side of the chicken and turn over to brown the other side. Cook the chicken in two batches if necessary.

2. Turn the chicken skin side up and add the garlic, wine, broth, salt, and pepper. Bring to the boil, cover the pan, and allow to simmer over a gentle heat for about 30-35 minutes.

3. Add the zucchini and cook for 10 minutes. Once the chicken and zucchini are done, add the olives and cook to heat through. Add the parsley and remove to a dish to serve.

TIME: Preparation takes about 25 minutes, cooking takes about 50-55 minutes.

SERVING IDEAS: Serve with rice or pasta and tomato salad.

VARIATIONS: Artichoke hearts may be used in place of the zucchini.

CHICKEN WITH MANGO

The exotic flavors of mango and spices make a lovely combination in this dish.

SERVES 4

---

2 tbsps oil
1 tsp grated ginger
½ tsp ground cinnamon
4 chicken breasts, shredded
4 green onions, sliced diagonally
1 tbsp light soy sauce
1 chicken soup cube
⅔ cup water
1 tsp sugar
Salt and pepper
2 ripe mangoes, peeled and sliced, or 1 can
   sliced mangoes, drained
2 tbsps sherry

1. Heat a wok and add the oil. Add the ginger and cinnamon, and sauté for 30 seconds.

2. Add the chicken and green onions, and stir-fry for 5 minutes.

3. Add the light soy sauce, crumbled soup cube, water, and sugar, and bring to the boil.

4. Add salt and pepper to taste, and simmer for 15 minutes.

5. Add the mangoes and sherry, and simmer, uncovered, until the sauce has reduced and thickened.

TIME: Preparation takes about 10 minutes and cooking takes about 30 minutes.

PREPARATION: To cut up a fresh mango, first remove the peel then cut off the two rounded sides either side of the large flat stone.

SERVING IDEAS: Serve with boiled rice and snow-peas.

Poulet Grillé au Citron Vert

Crisp chicken with a tang of limes makes an elegant yet quickly-made entrée. From the warm regions of southern France, it is perfect for a summer meal.

SERVES 4

---

2 × 2-pound chickens
1 tsp chopped fresh basil
6 tbsps olive oil
4 limes
Salt, pepper, and sugar

---

1. Remove the leg ends, neck, and wing tips from the chickens and discard them.

2. Split the chickens in half, cutting away the backbone completely and discarding it.

3. Loosen the ball-and-socket joint in the leg and flatten each half of the chickens by hitting them with the flat side of a cleaver.

4. Season the chickens on both sides with salt and pepper and sprinkle with the basil. Place the chickens in a shallow dish and pour 2 tbsps of olive oil over. Squeeze the juice from 2 of the limes over the chicken.

Cover and leave to marinate in the refrigerator for 4 hours or overnight.

5. Heat the broiler to its highest setting and preheat the oven to 375°F. Remove the chicken from the marinade and place in the broiler pan. Cook one side until golden-brown and turn the pieces over. Sprinkle with 1 tbsp olive oil and brown the other side.

6. Place the chicken in a roasting tin, sprinkle with the remaining oil, and roast in the oven for about 25 minutes. Cut the peel from the remaining limes, removing all the white parts, and slice them thinly. When the chicken is cooked, place the lime slices on top, and sprinkle lightly with sugar. Place under the broiler for a few minutes to caramelize the sugar and cook the limes. Place the chickens in a serving dish and spoon any remaining marinade over them with the cooking juices. Serve immediately.

TIME: Preparation takes about 25 minutes, plus 4 hours marinating, cooking takes about 35 minutes.

WATCHPOINT: Sugar will burn and turn bitter quickly, so watch carefully while broiling.

VARIATIONS: If you can get limes fresh from the tree, use the lime leaves instead of basil, or use fresh lemons and lemon leaves.

Chicken and Avocado Salad

The creamy herb dressing complements this easy summer salad.

SERVES 4

8 anchovy fillets, soaked in milk, rinsed, and dried

1 green, onion, chopped

2 tbsps chopped fresh tarragon

3 tbsps chopped chives

4 tbsps minced parsley

⅔ cup mayonnaise

⅔ cup plain yogurt

2 tbsps tarragon vinegar

Pinch each sugar and cayenne pepper

1 large head lettuce

4 cups cooked chicken strips or cubes

1 avocado, peeled, and sliced or cubed coated with 1 tbsp lemon juice

1. Combine all the ingredients, except the lettuce, chicken and avocado in a food processor. Blend the ingredients until smooth, and well-mixed. Leave in the refrigerator at least 1 hour for the flavors to blend.

2. Shred the lettuce or tear into bite-size pieces and arrange on plates.

3. Top the lettuce with the cooked chicken cut into strips or cubes.

4. Spoon the dressing over the chicken and garnish the salad with the avocado. Serve any remaining dressing separately.

TIME: Preparation takes about 30 minutes plus 1 hour refrigeration for the dressing.

PREPARATION: Dressing may be prepared ahead of time and kept in the refrigerator for a day or two.

POULET FRICASSÉE

This is a white stew, enriched and thickened with an egg-and-cream mixture which is called a liaison.

SERVES 4

4 tbsps butter or margarine

1 × 3-pound chicken, quartered and
   skinned

2 tbsps flour

2½ cups chicken broth

Grated rind and juice of ½ lemon

1 bouquet garni (parsley, bayleaf, thyme)

12-16 pearl onions, peeled

3 cups button mushrooms, whole if small,
   quartered if large

2 egg yolks

6 tbsps heavy cream

3 tbsps milk (optional)

Salt and pepper

2 tbsps minced parsley and thyme

Lemon slices to garnish

1. Melt 3 tbsps of the butter in a large skillet. Add the chicken in one layer and cook over gentle heat for about 5 minutes, or until the chicken is no longer pink. Do not allow the chicken to brown. If necessary, cook the chicken in two batches. When the chicken is sufficiently cooked, remove it from the pan and set aside.

2. Stir the flour into the butter remaining in the pan and cook over very low heat, stirring continuously for about 1 minute, or until pale straw in color. Remove the pan from the heat and gradually beat in the chicken broth. When blended smoothly, add lemon rind and juice, return the pan to the heat, and bring to the boil, whisking constantly. Reduce the heat and allow the sauce to simmer for 1 minute.

3. Return the chicken to the pan with any juices that have accumulated, and add the bouquet garni. The sauce should almost cover the chicken. If it does not, add more broth or water. Bring to the boil, cover the pan, and reduce the heat. Allow the chicken to simmer gently for 30 minutes.

4. Meanwhile, melt the remaining butter in a small skillet, add the onions, cover, and cook very gently for 10 minutes. Do not allow the onions to brown. Remove the onions from the pan with a slotted spoon and add to the chicken. Cook the mushrooms in the remaining butter for 2 minutes. Set the mushrooms aside and add them to the chicken 10 minutes before the end of cooking.

5. Test the chicken by piercing a thigh portion with a sharp knife. If the juices run clear, the chicken is cooked. Transfer chicken and vegetables to a serving plate and discard the bouquet garni. Skim any fat from the sauce and boil it rapidly to reduce by almost half.

6. Blend the egg yolks and cream together and whisk in several spoonfuls of the hot sauce. Return the egg yolk and cream mixture to the remaining sauce and cook gently for 2-3 minutes. Stir the sauce constantly and do not allow it to boil. If very thick, add milk. Adjust the seasoning and stir in the parsley and thyme. Place the chicken in a serving dish and spoon the sauce over it. Garnish with lemon slices.

PECAN CHICKEN

Pecans can be used in both sweet and savory dishes. Here, their rich, sweet taste complements a stuffing for chicken.

SERVES 4

4 boned chicken breasts

3 tbsps butter or margarine

1 small onion, minced

⅓ cup pork sausagemeat

⅔ cup fresh breadcrumbs

1 tsp chopped thyme

1 tsp minced parsley

1 small egg, lightly beaten

½ cup pecan halves

1¼ cups chicken broth

1 tbsp all-purpose flour

2 tbsps sherry

Salt and pepper

Chopped parsley or 1 bunch watercress to garnish

1. Cut a small pocket in the thick side of each chicken breast, using a small knife.

2. Melt 1 tbsp of the butter in a small saucepan and add the onion. Cook for a few minutes over gentle heat to soften. Add the sausagemeat and turn up the heat to brown. Break up the sausagemeat with a fork as it cooks.

3. Drain off any excess fat, and add the breadcrumbs, herbs, and a pinch of salt and pepper. Allow to cool slightly and add enough egg to hold the mixture together. Chop the pecans, reserving 8 of them, and add to the stuffing.

4. Using a small teaspoon, fill the pocket in each chicken breast with some of the stuffing.

5. Melt another tbsp of the butter in a casserole and add the chicken breasts, skin side downward. Brown over moderate heat and turn over. Brown the other side quickly to seal.

6. Add the broth, cover the casserole, and cook for about 25-30 minutes in a preheated 350°F oven until tender.

7. When the chicken is cooked, remove it to a serving platter to keep warm. Reserve the cooking liquid.

8. Melt the remaining butter in a small saucepan and stir in the flour. Cook to a pale straw color. Strain the cooking liquid over it and add the sherry. Bring to the boil and stir constantly until thickened. Add the reserved pecans and seasoning.

9. Spoon some of the sauce over the chicken. Garnish with chopped parsley or a bunch of watercress.

TIME: Preparation takes about 30 minutes and cooking takes about 40 minutes.

VARIATIONS: Almonds, butternuts, hicory nuts or macadamias can be used instead. Crush macadamias roughly for the garnish and brown lightly in the butter before adding flour for the sauce.

SERVING IDEAS: Serve with a rice or sauté potatoes.

Poulet Sauté Vallée d'Auge

This dish contains all the ingredients that Normandy is famous for – butter, cream, apples, and Calvados.

SERVES 4

4 tbsps butter or margarine

2 tbsps oil

1 × 3-pound chicken, cut into 8 portions

4 tbsps Calvados

6 tbsps chicken broth

2 apples, peeled, cored, and coarsely chopped

1 shallot, minced

2 sticks celery, finely chopped

½ tsp dried thyme, crumbled

2 egg yolks, lightly beaten

6 tbsps heavy cream

Salt and white pepper

Garnish

2 tbsps butter

2 apples, quartered, cored, and cut into cubes

Sugar

1 bunch watercress or small parsley sprigs

1. Heat half the butter and all of the oil in a large skillet over moderate heat. When the foam begins to subside, brown the chicken, a few pieces at a time, skin side downward, then turn it. When all the chicken is browned, pour off most of the fat from the pan and return the chicken to the pan.

2. Pour the Calvados into a small saucepan and warm over gentle heat. Ignite with a match and pour, while still flaming, over the chicken. Shake the skillet gently until the flames subside. If the Calvados should flare up, cover the pan immediately with the lid.

3. Remove the chicken from the pan and reserve it in a warm place. Pour the broth into the skillet and scrape any browned chicken juices from the bottom.

4. Melt the remaining butter in a small saucepan or skillet. Cook the chopped apples, shallot, celery, and the thyme for about 10 minutes or until soft but not browned.

5. Combine the apple mixture with the broth. Place the chicken in a Dutch oven or casserole and pour the sauce over it. Place on high heat. Bring to the boil, then reduce heat, cover the pan and simmer for 50 minutes.

6. When the chicken is cooked, beat the eggs and cream. With a whisk, gradually beat in some of the hot chicken cooking liquid. Pour the mixture back into a saucepan and cook over a low heat for 2-3 minutes, stirring constantly until the sauce thickens and coats the back of a spoon.

7. Season the sauce with salt and white pepper, and set aside.

8. To make the garnish, melt the butter in a small skillet and when foaming, add the apple. Toss over a high heat until beginning to soften. Sprinkle with sugar, and cook until the apple begins to caramelize.

9. To serve, coat the chicken with the sauce and decorate with watercress or parsley. Spoon the caramelized apples over the chicken.

Tarragon Chicken Pancakes

These attractive pancakes look sophisticated enough for a dinner party, but are so easy to make, you can indulge yourself at any time.

SERVES 4

1 cup whole-wheat flour
1 egg
1¼ cups milk
Oil for frying
3 tbsps butter
3 tbsps all-purpose flour
1¼ cups milk
Salt and black pepper, to taste
1 cup chopped, cooked chicken
1 avocado peeled, halved, pitted, and
    chopped
2 tsps lemon juice
1 tbsp chopped fresh tarragon

1. Put the whole-wheat flour into a large bowl, and make a slight well in the center. Break the egg into the well and begin to beat the egg carefully into the flour, incorporating only a little flour at a time.

2. Add the milk gradually to the egg-and-flour mixture, beating well between additions, until all the milk is incorporated and the mixture is smooth.

3. Heat a little oil in a small skillet, or crêpe pan, and cook about 2 tbsps of the mixture at a time, tipping and rotating the pan, so that it spreads evenly over the base to form a pancake. Flip the pancake over, to cook the other side.

4. Repeat this process until all the mixture has been used. Keep the pancakes warm, until required.

5. Melt the butter in a small saucepan, stir in the flour, and cook over a medium heat for 1-2 minutes. Remove from the heat and gradually stir in the milk. Bring to the boil, stirring, then simmer for 1-2 minutes. Season to taste.

6. Stir the chopped chicken, avocado, lemon juice, and tarragon into the sauce.

7. Fold each pancake in half, and then in half again, to form a triangle.

8. Carefully open part of the triangle out to form an envelope, and fill this with the chicken and avocado mixture.

TIME: Preparation takes about 25 minutes, and cooking takes about 25 minutes.

SERVING IDEAS: Serve piping hot, garnished with watercress and accompany with a crisp green salad.

CORNISH GAME HENS IN CURRY SAUCE

Whole roast Cornish game hens served with a spicy sauce makes a nice alternative to the usual curry.

SERVES 4

¼ cup butter
1 tsp oil
4 Cornish game hens
1 medium onion, finely chopped
1 clove garlic, crushed
2 tsps curry powder
⅔ cup chicken broth
Squeeze of lemon juice
2 tsps mango chutney
1 tbsp yellow raisins
2 tsps cornstarch
Cold water

---

1. Put butter and the oil in a roasting pan and place in an oven preheated to 350°F. When sizzling, remove from the oven, add the Cornish game hens and baste well.

Return the pan to the oven and roast the birds for about 35 minutes, basting at regular intervals until they are cooked. Test with a skewer inserted into the thickest part of the leg. If the liquid runs clear, the Cornish game hens are cooked. Remove from the roasting pan and keep them warm.

2. Drain off any excess fat from the pan and place it over a medium heat. Add the chopped onion and garlic, and sauté for a few minutes until softened. Reduce the heat, add the curry powder, and stir well for 2-3 minutes. Add the chicken broth and stir until it is bubbling. Add the squeeze of lemon juice, chutney, and yellow raisins.

3. In a cup, blend the cornstarch with a little cold water and add it to the sauce. Mix well and cook for a few more minutes. Pour over the Cornish game hens or serve separately.

TIME: Preparation takes about 10 minutes and cooking takes about 40 minutes.

VARIATIONS: Substitute other sweet pickles for mango chutney for a different flavor.

SERVING IDEAS: Serve with Indian breads and rice.

Niçoise Chicken

The combination of fresh herbs, tomatoes, and black olives brings the taste of Provence to your table.

SERVES 4

4 boned chicken breasts, unskinned

4 tbsps oil

2 tbsps lemon juice

Tapenade filling

4 cups large black olives, pitted

2 tbsps capers

1 clove garlic, coarsely chopped

4 anchovy fillets

2 tbsps olive oil

Raw tomato sauce

4 cups ripe tomatoes, skinned, de-seeded, and chopped

1 shallot, very finely chopped

2 tbsps minced parsley

2 tbsps chopped basil

2 tbsps white wine vinegar

2 tbsps olive oil

1 tbsp sugar

Salt and pepper

1 tbsp tomato paste (optional)

1. Cut a pocket in the thickest side of the chicken breasts.

2. Combine half the olives, half the capers, and the remaining ingredients for the tapenade in a blender or food processor. Work to a purée.

3. Add the remaining olives and capers and process a few times to chop them coarsely.

4. Fill the chicken breasts with the tapenade. Chill, to help filling to become firm.

5. Combine the oil and lemon juice and baste the skin side. Cook skin side down first for 10 minutes under a pre-heated medium-hot broiler. Turn over, baste again, and broil for another 10 minutes on the other side or until tender.

6. Meanwhile, combine the tomato sauce ingredients, and mix very well. Serve with the chicken.

TIME: Preparation takes about 30 minutes and cooking takes about 20 minutes.

PREPARATION: Both the filling and sauce can be made in advance and kept refrigerated.

SERVING IDEAS: Serve with new potatoes and small green beans.

POUSSINS ESPAGNOLES

The olive oil in this recipe gives a wonderful flavor to the sauce.

SERVES 4

4 Cornish game hens
Salt and freshly ground black pepper
Olive oil, to brush
4 small wedges of lime or lemon
4 bayleaves
2 tbsps olive oil
1 small onion, thinly sliced
1 clove garlic, crushed
1 pound tomatoes
⅔ cup red wine
⅔ cup chicken or vegetable broth
1 tbsp tomato paste
1 green chili, seeded and thinly sliced
1 small red bell pepper, cut into thin strips
1 small green bell pepper, cut into thin strips
2 tbsps chopped, blanched almonds
1 tbsp pinenuts
12 small black olives, pitted
1 tbsp raisins

1. Rub the Cornish game hens inside and out with salt and pepper. Brush the skins with olive oil and push a wedge of lemon or lime, and a bayleaf into the cavity of each one.

2. Roast the Cornish game hens uncovered, in a preheated 375°F oven for 45 minutes, or until just tender.

3. Meanwhile, heat the 2 tbsps olive oil in a large skillet and gently cook the onion and the garlic until they are soft, but not colored.

4. Cut a slit into the skins of each tomato and plunge into boiling water for 30 seconds.

5. Using a sharp knife, carefully peel away the skins from the blanched tomatoes.

6. Chop the tomatoes coarsely. Remove and discard the seeds and cores.

7. Add the chopped tomatoes to the cooked onion and garlic, and fry gently for a further 2 minutes.

8. Add all the remaining ingredients and simmer for 10-15 minutes, or until the tomatoes have completely softened, and the sauce has thickened slightly.

9. Arrange the Cornish game hens on a serving dish and spoon a little of the sauce over each one.

10. Serve hot and hand the remaining sauce in a gravy-boat.

TIME: Preparation takes 15 minutes, cooking takes about 45 minutes.

SERVING IDEAS: Serve with rice and a mixed green salad.

COOK'S TIP: If the Cornish game hens start to get too brown during the cooking time, cover them lightly with aluminum foil.

285

Contents

Introduction

Fish and seafood are among our most valuable natural assets. They are high in easily digestible protein, low in fat, offer endless variety and are quick and easy to cook. The popularity of fish and seafood has waned in the recent past due to its unjustified reputation for being difficult to prepare. Today, however, people acknowledge that although it needs a little preparation, this is mostly very straightforward and is well worth the effort. And, of course, if you don't want to put in any effort, the selection of ready-prepared fresh and frozen fish in the supermarket grows larger every year.

Better refrigeration techniques have meant more and more consumers can now enjoy varieties of fish and seafood that once would have been considered very exotic. And unusual fish, that would once have been impossible to find, are now regularly available at supermarkets. The most important thing to bear in mind when buying fish and seafood is freshness. Buy the freshest produce you possibly can and you will not go wrong. Find a source that has a very high turnover and examine the produce carefully before you buy it. If it is fish, it should not smell "fishy" as this means it is past its best. It should be moist, the flesh firm and the eyes bright. Seafood, too, should be firm, have a good color and look moist and fresh.

Cooking fish and seafood is much more simple than many people imagine and it has the added advantage of being quick to cook. The essential point to remember is never to overcook fish and seafood as it quickly loses its lovely tasty juiciness. The best way to treat it, therefore, is to combine it with ingredients and sauces that enhance, rather than mask, this fresh flavor. It is for this reason that stuffed fish dishes are so popular – all the flavor of the fish is to the fore with a little stuffing to add extra "bite." Mixing fish and seafood in chowders is also wonderful as a whole variety of flavors such as crab, shrimp and mussels can be blended with your own favorite flavorings to create a dish that is completely original!

The recipes in this book highlight some of the tastiest recipes for fish and seafood, whether for a simple lunch dish or a family meal, but they should also inspire the cook to experiment with the expanded range of fish and seafood now available.

MUSSEL SOUP

Shellfish contain a multitude of vitamins and minerals, especially vitamins A, E, D and K, and this soup is a delicious way of making sure you have a good supply of all of these.

SERVES 4

3 quarts fresh mussels
¼ cup butter
2 onions, peeled and finely chopped
2 cloves garlic, crushed
1¼ cups dry white wine
1¼ cups water
2 tbsps lemon juice
2 oz fresh white bread crumbs
2 tbsps parsley, freshly chopped
Salt and freshly ground black pepper

1. Scrub the mussels with a stiff brush and remove any barnacle shells or pieces of seaweed that are attached to them.

2. Tap each mussel sharply to make sure that it closes tightly.

3. Melt the butter in a large saucepan and gently fry the onions and garlic until they are soft, but not browned.

4. Add the mussels, wine, water and lemon juice to the pan, and bring to a boil. Season with salt and pepper, then cover and cook for approximately 10 minutes or until all the mussel shells have completely opened.

5. Discard any mussels which have not opened fully.

6. Strain the mussels through a colander and return the juices and stock to the saucepan. Put the mussels in a serving dish and keep warm.

7. Add the bread crumbs and the parsley to the mussel juices and bring them to the boil. Adjust the seasoning, and pour over the mussels. Serve immediately.

TIME Preparation takes 15 minutes, cooking takes approximately 20 minutes.

WATCHPOINT When cooking fresh mussels, great care must be taken to ensure that they are safe to eat. Discard any that do not shut tightly before cooking, or do not open after cooking.

HOT AND SOUR SEAFOOD SOUP

This interesting combination of flavors and ingredients makes a sophisticated beginning to an informal meal.

SERVES 4

3 dried Chinese mushrooms
1 tbsp vegetable oil
¾ cup shrimp, shelled and deveined
1 red chili, seeded and finely sliced
1 green chili, seeded and finely sliced
½ tsp lemon rind, cut into thin slivers
2 green onions, sliced
2½ cups fish stock
1 tbsp Worcestershire sauce
1 tbsp light soy sauce
2 oz whitefish fillets
1 cake of fresh bean curd, diced
1 tbsp lemon juice
1 tsp sesame seeds
Salt and pepper
1 tsp fresh coriander, finely chopped
(optional)

1. Soak the mushrooms in enough hot water to cover for 20 minutes, or until completely reconstituted.

2. Heat the vegetable oil in a large wok or frying pan, and add the shrimp, chilies, lemon rind and green onions. Stir-fry quickly for 1 minute.

3. Add the stock, the Worcestershire sauce and the soy sauce. Bring this mixture to a boil, reduce the heat and simmer for 5 minutes. Season to taste.

4. Remove the hard stalks from the mushrooms and discard them. Slice the caps very finely.

5. Cut the whitefish fillets into small dice, and add them to the soup, together with the bean curd and Chinese mushrooms. Simmer for a further 5 minutes.

6. Stir in the lemon juice and sesame seeds. Adjust the seasoning and serve sprinkled with chopped fresh coriander leaves, if desired.

TIME Preparation takes about 20 minutes, cooking takes about 20 minutes.

COOK'S TIP If you cannot buy coriander use parsley instead.

CHILLED SHRIMP, AVOCADO AND CUCUMBER SOUP

Avocado and cucumber give this soup its pretty color.

SERVES 4

8 oz unpeeled shrimp
1 large ripe avocado
1 cucumber
1 small bunch dill
Juice of half a lemon
1¼ cups chicken stock
2½ cups plain yogurt
Salt and pepper

1. Peel all the shrimp, reserving the shells. Add shells to chicken stock and bring to a boil. Allow to simmer for about 15 minutes. Cool and strain.

2. Peel the avocado and cut it into pieces. Cut 8 thin slices from the cucumber and peel the rest. Remove seeds and chop the cucumber coarsely.

3. Put the avocado and cucumber into a food processor or blender and process until smooth. Add a squeeze of lemon juice, and pour on the cold chicken stock.

4. Reserve a sprig of dill for garnish, and add the rest to the mixture in the processor and blend again.

5. Add about 1½ cups of yogurt to the processor and blend until smooth. Add salt and pepper. Stir in the peeled shrimp by hand, reserving a few as garnish.

6. Chill the soup well. Serve in individual bowls, garnished with a spoonful of yogurt, a sprig of dill, and thinly sliced rounds of cucumber.

TIME Preparation takes 15 minutes, cooking takes 15 minutes.

CRABMEAT BALLS

Delicious an appetizer or a cocktail snack, crabmeat balls can be made ahead, then coated and fried at the last minute.

SERVES 6-8

1 lb fresh or frozen crabmeat, chopped
    finely
4 slices white bread, crusts removed and
    made into crumbs
1 tbsp butter or margarine
1 tbsp flour
½ cub milk
½ red or green chili, seeded and finely
    chopped
1 green onion, finely chopped
1 tbsp chopped parsley
Salt
Flour
2 eggs, beaten
Dry bread crumbs
Oil for frying

1. Combine the crabmeat with the fresh bread crumbs and set aside.

2. Melt the butter and add the flour off the heat. Stir in the milk and return to moderate heat. Bring to a boil, stirring constantly.

3. Stir the white sauce into the crabmeat and bread crumbs, adding the chili, onion and parsley. Season with salt to taste, cover and allow to cool completely.

4. Shape the cold mixture into 1 inch balls with floured hands.

5. Coat with beaten egg using a fork to turn balls in the mixture or use a pastry brush to coat with egg.

6. Coat with the dry bread crumbs.

7. Fry in oil in a deep frying pan, saucepan or deep-fat fryer at 350°F until golden brown and crisp, about 3 minutes per batch of 6. Turn occasionally while frying.

8. Drain on paper towels and sprinkle lightly with salt.

TIME Preparation takes about 40-50 minutes, including time for the mixture to cool. A batch of 6 balls takes about 3 minutes to cook.

MUSSELS MARINIÈRE

Brittany and Normandy are famous for mussels and for cream and so cooks combined the two in one perfect seafood dish.

SERVES 4

3 quarts mussels
1½ cups white wine
4 shallots, finely chopped
1 clove garlic, crushed
1 bouquet garni
½ cup heavy cream
3 tbsps butter, cut into small pieces
2 tbsps fresh parsley, finely chopped
Salt and pepper

1. Scrub the mussels well and remove the beards and any barnacles from the shells. Discard any mussels that have cracked shells and do not close when tapped. Put the mussels into a large bowl and soak in cold water for at least 1 hour. Meanwhile, chop the parsley very finely.

2. Bring the wine to the boil in a large saucepan and add the shallots, garlic and bouquet garni. Add the mussels, cover the pan and cook for 5 minutes. Shake the pan or stir the mussels around frequently until the shells open. Lift out the mussels into a large soup tureen or individual serving bowls. Discard any mussels that have not opened.

3. Reduce the cooking liquid by about half and strain into another saucepan. Add the cream and bring to the boil to thicken slightly. Beat in the butter, a few pieces at a time. Season to taste, add the parsley and pour the sauce over the mussels to serve.

TIME Preparation takes about 30 minutes, cooking takes about 15 minutes.

SERVING IDEAS Serve as a first course with French bread, or double the quantity of mussels to serve for a light main course.

FISH TEMPURA

This is a traditional Japanese dish, which can be served as an unusual appetizer.

SERVES 4

12 uncooked large shrimp
2 whitefish fillets, skinned and cut into
    2 ¾-inch strips
Small whole fish, e.g. smelt or whitebait
2 squid, cleaned and cut into 3-inch strips
2 tbsps all-purpose flour
1 egg yolk
½ cup iced water
1 cup all-purpose flour
Oil for frying
6 tbsps soy sauce
Juice and finely grated rind of 2 limes
4 tbsps dry sherry

1. Shell the shrimp, leaving the tails intact. Wash the fish and the squid and pat dry. Sprinkle them all with the 2 tbsps flour.

2. Make a batter by beating together the egg yolk and water. Sieve in the 1 cup of flour and mix in well with a knife.

3. Dip each piece of fish into the batter, shaking off any excess.

4. In a wok or deep-fat fryer, heat the oil to 350°F. Lower in the fish pieces a few at a time and cook for 2-3 minutes. Lift them out carefully and drain on paper towels, keeping warm until required.

5. Mix together the soy sauce, lime juice, rind and sherry and serve as a dip with the cooked fish.

TIME Preparation takes about 30 minutes, cooking time varies from 2 to 3 minutes depending on the type of fish.

VARIATIONS Use a few vegetables, as well as fish, for an interesting change. Whole mushrooms are especially good.

SALMON PÂTÉ

This highly nutritious, elegant pâté is low in fat and very quick to prepare.

SERVES 4

---

8 oz can red or pink salmon, drained
½ cup low fat cottage cheese
Few drops lemon juice
Pinch ground mace, or ground nutmeg
¼ tsp Tabasco sauce
Freshly ground sea salt and black pepper
2 tbsps low fat plain yogurt
4 small pickles

---

1. Remove any bones and skin from the salmon. In a bowl, work the fish into a smooth paste with the back of a spoon.

2. Beat the cottage cheese until it is smooth.

3. Add the salmon, lemon juice, seasonings, and yogurt to the cheese and mix well, until thoroughly incorporated.

4. Divide the mixture equally among 4 individual ramekins. Smooth the surfaces carefully.

5. Slice each pickle lengthways, 4 or 5 times, making sure that you do not cut completely through the pickle at the narrow end. Splay the cut ends into a fan, and use these to decorate the tops of the pâtés in the ramekins.

TIME Preparation takes about 15 minutes.

PREPARATION If you have a food processor or blender you can work the cheese and salmon together in this, instead of beating them in a bowl.

DRESSED CRAB

No book on fish cookery would be complete without instructions on how to dress a crab. Crabs should have rough shells, large claws and feel heavy for their size. Do not buy a crab that sounds to have water in when shaken.

SERVES 2-3

1 large cooked crab (see note)
Chopped fresh parsley, to garnish

1. Pull off the crab claws, and crack these with a small hammer or nutcrackers. Pull out the meat and put into a bowl for light meat.

2. Turn the crab onto its back or uppermost shell, and pull the underbody firmly away from the main shell.

3. Remove and discard the stomach bag and gray, feathered gills, or fingers, as these must not be eaten. Scoop out the dark meat from the shell with a spoon and put into a bowl.

4. Crack open the underbody and remove all the white meat with a skewer or fork. Put into the appropriate bowl.

5. Remove enough of the top shell to make a flat case, in which to serve the meat. Scrub the shell thoroughly.

6. Arrange layers of dark and light meat alternately in the shell, and garnish with the parsley.

TIME Preparation takes about 35-45 minutes.

SERVING IDEAS Serve with new potatoes and a simple, mixed lettuce salad.

PREPARATION To cook a hard-shell crab, place crab in a saucepan of boiling, salted water, reduce heat and simmer for 20-25 minutes.

MATELOTE

A tasty, impressive dish perfect for entertaining.

SERVES 4

1 lb lemon sole
1 lb monkfish
1 small wing of skate
4 cups mussels
8 oz unpeeled shrimp
3 onions
⅓ cup butter
2 cups white wine
¼ cup flour
2 tbsps parsley, chopped
Salt
Freshly ground black pepper
Lemon juice

1. Fillet and skin the lemon sole. Cut the sole fillets and monkfish into large pieces. Chop the skate wing into 4 large pieces.

2. Peel the shrimp and set aside. Scrub the mussels well, discarding any with broken shells.

3. Chop the onion finely. Melt half the butter in a saucepan and soften the onion in a large saucepan.

4. Add the mussels and about 3-4 tbsps water. Cover the pan and shake over a high heat until all the mussels have opened, discarding any that have not.

5. Strain the liquid into a bowl, allow mussels to cool, and then shell them.

6. Return the cooking liquid to the saucepan. Place the pieces of fish in the liquid. Add the wine until it just covers the fish. Simmer gently for about 8 minutes or until fish is just cooked.

7. Mix together the flour and the remaining butter to make a paste.

8. Remove the cooked fish from the liquid and put into a serving dish to keep warm. Bring liquid to a boil. Add the flour and butter paste, a little at a time, whisking it in and allowing liquid to boil after each addition, until liquid is thickened.

9. Add the parsley, shelled shrimp, shelled mussels, a little lemon juice, and seasoning. Heat for a few minutes to warm the shellfish through. Pour over the fish in the serving dish and sprinkle with more chopped parsley if desired.

TIME Preparation takes 20 minutes, cooking takes 20 minutes.

Mussels alla Genovese

Mussels Italian style – the perfect start to any meal.

SERVES 4

---

3 lbs mussels
Juice of 1 lemon
1 shallot
1 handful fresh basil leaves, or 1 tsp dried
    basil
1 small bunch parsley
¼ cup walnut halves
1 clove garlic
2 tbsps freshly grated Parmesan cheese
3-6 tbsps olive oil
2 tbsps butter
Salt and pepper
Flour or oatmeal

Garnish
Fresh basil leaves

---

1. Scrub the mussels well and discard any with broken shells or those that do not close when tapped. Put the mussels into a bowl of clean water with a handful of flour or oatmeal. Leave for ½ hour, then rinse under clear water.

2. Chop the shallot finely and put into a large saucepan with lemon juice. Cook until shallot softens.

3. Add the mussels and a pinch of salt and pepper. Cover the pan and cook the mussels quickly, shaking the pan. When mussel shells have opened, take mussels out of the pan, set aside and keep warm. Discard any that do not open. Strain the cooking liquid for possible use later.

4. To prepare Genovese sauce, wash the basil leaves, if fresh, and parsley, peel the garlic clove and chop coarsely, and chop the walnuts coarsely.

5. Put the herbs, garlic, nuts, 1 tbsp grated cheese and salt and pepper into a food processor and work to chop coarsely. Add butter and work again. Turn machine on and add oil gradually through the feed tube. If the sauce is still too thick, add the reserved liquid from cooking the mussels.

6. Remove the top shells from mussels and discard. Arrange mussels evenly in 4 shallow dishes, spoon some of the sauce into each, and sprinkle the top lightly with remaining Parmesan cheese.

7. Garnish with basil leaves and serve.

TIME Preparation takes 15 minutes, cooking takes 5-8 minutes.

311

CRAB AND CITRUS SALAD

This delicious salad is perfect for a summer lunch.

SERVES 4

8 oz crabmeat, or 1 large crab
2 oranges
2 lemons
2 limes
1 pink grapefruit
1 small iceberg lettuce
½ cup plain yogurt
6 tbsps heavy cream
1 tbsp chili sauce
½ tbsp brandy
Pinch of cayenne pepper
Salt
2 tbsps salad oil

1. Separate the body from the shell of the whole crab, and remove and discard the lungs and stomach sac. Chop body into 3 or 4 pieces with a very sharp knife and pick out the meat. Scrape brown meat from inside shell and add to body meat.

2. Break off large claws and remove meat from legs; then crack the claws and remove claw meat.

3. Mix all the meat together and reserve legs for garnish. If using canned or frozen crabmeat, pick over the meat to remove any bits of shell or cartilage.

4. Mix together yogurt, chili sauce, cream, brandy, cayenne pepper and a pinch of salt, and toss with the crabmeat.

5. Take a thin strip of peel from each of the citrus fruits, scraping off the bitter white pith. Cut each strip of peel into thin slivers. Put into boiling water and allow to boil for about 1 minute. Drain, refresh under cold water, and set aside.

6. Peel each of the citrus fruits and cut into segments; do all this over a bowl to reserve juices.

7. Add 2 tbsps salad oil to the juice in the bowl, and toss with citrus segments. Shred iceberg lettuce and arrange on plates. Put the crabmeat in its dressing on top of lettuce.

8. Arrange citrus segments over and around crabmeat and sprinkle citrus peel over the top.

TIME Preparation takes about 20 minutes.

SOUR FRIED SEAFOOD

A fragrant sour fried curry from the Far East. This can be served on its own, or as one of a combination of dishes.

SERVES 4

1 lb mixed fish and seafood, to include any of the following: large shrimp; scallops; squid, cleaned and cut into rings; oysters, shelled; clams, shelled; crab claws, shelled; small whole fish, e.g. whitebait or smelt.

½ cup oil

1 tbsp fresh ginger, grated

4 shallots, finely chopped

3 cloves garlic, crushed

4 red chili peppers, seeded and finely chopped

1 tsp ground mace

½ tsp shrimp paste

1 piece tamarind, soaked in 4 tbsps hot water (see variation)

Pinch soft brown sugar

Salt

1. Heat the oil in a frying pan over a high heat. Fry the fish in several batches for 2-3 minutes per batch, or until lightly browned and cooked through. Drain on paper towels and keep warm.

2. Grind the shallots, ginger, garlic, chilies and mace to a smooth paste in a mortar and pestle. Add the shrimp paste and blend together well.

3. Put 1 tbsp of oil into a wok and add the spice paste. Cook gently for 2-3 minutes. Strain in the tamarind and water or lemon juice. The sauce should be of a thin coating consistency; add a little more water, if it is too thick.

4. Stir in the sugar, the cooked fish and salt to taste. Cook for 2-3 minutes, or until the fish is heated through.

TIME Preparation takes about 20 minutes, cooking takes about 12-15 minutes.

COOK'S TIP Great care should be taken when preparing fresh chilies. Always wash hands thoroughly afterwards, and avoid getting any neat juice in the eyes or mouth. Rinse with copious amounts of clear water if this happens.

VARIATION If tamarind is not available, substitute 2 tbsps of lemon juice.

SALMON AND VEGETABLE SALAD

The fish in this salad "cooks" in the refrigerator in its vinegar marinade. Insist on very fresh fish for this recipe.

SERVES 4

12 oz salmon fillets
2 carrots, peeled and diced
1 large zucchini, peeled and diced
1 large turnip, peeled and diced
Chopped fresh coriander or pinch of dried
3 tbsps tarragon or wine vinegar
Salt and pepper
Pinch cayenne pepper
3 tbsps olive oil
Whole coriander leaves to garnish

1. Skin the salmon fillet and cut the fish into 1 inch pieces. Place in a bowl and add the vinegar, stirring well. Leave to stand for at least 2 hours.

2. Cut the vegetables into ½ inch dice and place the carrots in a saucepan of boiling water for about 5 minutes. Add the zucchini and turnip during the last minute of cooking time. Drain well.

3. Add the coriander, oil, salt and pepper and pinch cayenne pepper to the fish. Combine with the vegetables, mixing carefully so the fish does not break up. Chill briefly before serving and garnish with fresh coriander if available.

TIME Preparation takes about 30 minutes, with 2 hours for the salmon to marinate.

COOK'S TIP Fish allowed to marinate in vinegar, lemon or lime juice will appear opaque and "cooked" after standing for about 2 hours.

FISHERMAN'S STEW

This quick, economical and satisfying fish dish will please any fish lover for lunch or a light supper.

SERVES 4-6

6 tbsps olive oil
2 large onions, sliced
1 red pepper, seeded and sliced
1½ cups mushrooms, sliced
16oz can tomatoes
Pinch salt and pepper
Pinch dried thyme
1¾ cups water
2 lbs cod or other whitefish fillets, skinned
¾ cup white wine
2 tbsps parsley, chopped

1. Heat the oil in a large saucepan and add the onions. Cook until beginning to look transluscent. Add the red pepper and cook until the vegetables are softened.

2. Add the mushrooms and the tomatoes and bring the mixture to a boil.

3. Add thyme, salt, pepper and water and simmer for about 30 minutes.

4. Add the fish and wine and cook until the fish flakes easily, about 15 minutes. Stir in parsley.

5. To serve, place a piece of toasted French bread in the bottom of the soup bowl and spoon over the fish stew.

TIME Preparation takes about 20 minutes, cooking takes about 45 minutes.

VARIATIONS Shellfish may be added with the fish, if desired. Substitute green peppers for red peppers.

SERVING IDEAS The stew may also be served over rice. Accompany with a green salad.

Salade Niçoise

This classic French salad is a meal in itself when served with a green salad and some crusty bread.

SERVES 4

2 large, or 6 small, new potatoes, cooked and cut into ½ inch dice

6 oz green beans, trimmed and cooked

3 oz black olives, halved and stoned

1 small cucumber, diced

4 tomatoes, cut into eight

6 oz can tuna, in water

¾ cup peeled shrimp

4 hard-cooked eggs, shelled and quartered lengthwise

2 oz can anchovies, drained and chopped

6 tbsps olive oil

2 tbsps white wine vinegar

3 tbsps chopped fresh mixed herbs or 1 tbsp dried

2 tsps Dijon mustard

Salt and pepper

1. In a large bowl, mix together the potatoes, beans, olives, cucumber and tomatoes.

2. Drain the tuna and flake it with a fork. Mix this, along with the shrimp, eggs and anchovies into the salad mixture.

3. In a small bowl, mix together the oil, vinegar, herbs and mustard. Whisk with a fork until thick.

4. Pour the dressing over the salad ingredients and stir gently to coat evenly. Season to taste.

TIME Preparation takes about 20 minutes, cooking takes about 20 minutes.

PREPARATION If you have a screw top jar, the dressing ingredients can be put into this and shaken vigorously, until they have thickened.

COOK'S TIP The dressing used in this recipe is delicious and will keep for up to 2 weeks in a refrigerator. So make double quantities and keep some to enliven other salad meals.

VARIATION If fresh herbs are not available substitute 1 tbsp dried mixed herbs.

COCONUT FRIED FISH WITH CHILIES

A real treat for lovers of spicy food.

SERVES 4

Oil for frying
1 lb sole or other white fish fillets, skinned, boned and cut into 1 inch strips
Seasoned flour
1 egg, beaten
¾ cup shredded coconut
1 tbsp vegetable oil
1 tsp fresh ginger, grated
¼ tsp chili powder
1 red chili, seeded and finely chopped
1 tsp ground coriander
½ tsp ground nutmeg
1 clove garlic, crushed
2 tbsps tomato paste
2 tbsps tomato chutney
2 tbsps dark soy sauce
2 tbsps lemon juice
2 tbsps water
1 tsp light brown sugar
Salt and pepper

1. In a frying pan, heat about 2 inches of oil to 375°F. Toss the fish strips in the seasoned flour and then dip them into the beaten egg. Roll them in the shredded coconut and shake off the excess.

2. Fry the fish, a few pieces at a time, in the hot oil and drain them on paper towels. Keep warm.

3. Heat the 1 tbsp oil in a wok or frying pan and fry the ginger, red chili, spices and garlic, for about 2 minutes.

4. Add the remaining ingredients and simmer for about 3 minutes. Serve the fish, with the sauce served separately.

TIME Preparation takes about 30 minutes, cooking takes about 30 minutes.

SERVING IDEAS Serve with plain boiled rice, a cucumber relish and plenty of salad.

SWORDFISH KEBABS

Swordfish won't fall apart during cooking – a bonus when making kebabs.

SERVES 4-6

2¼ lbs swordfish steaks
6 tbsps olive oil
1 tsp chopped fresh oregano or ½ tsp dried
1 tsp chopped fresh marjoram or ½ tsp dried
Juice and rind of ½ lemon
4 tomatoes, cut in thick slices, or cherry tomatoes
2 lemons, cut in thin slices
Salt and freshly ground pepper
Lemon slices and Italian flat leaf parsley for garnish

1. Cut the swordfish steaks into 2 inch pieces.

2. Mix the olive oil, herbs, lemon juice and rind, and seasoning together and set it aside. Thread the swordfish, tomato slices or cherry tomatoes and lemon slices on skewers, alternating the ingredients. Brush the skewers with the oil and lemon juice mixture and cook under a preheated broiler for about 10 minutes, basting frequently with the lemon and oil. Serve garnished with lemons and parsley.

TIME Preparation takes about 15 minutes, cooking takes about 10 minutes.

VARIATIONS Fresh tuna may be used instead of swordfish.

SERVING IDEAS Accompany the kebabs with risotto and a green salad.

VINEGARED CRAB

An unusual way of serving fresh crab. You should be able to buy the rice vinegar from a supermarket or health food store. If not, substitute white wine vinegar.

SERVES 4

1 cucumber, grated
Salt, for sprinkling
1 large cooked crab
1 small piece fresh ginger, grated
Chinese cabbage, for serving
3 tbsps rice vinegar
2 tbsps dry sherry
2 tbsps soy sauce

1. Sprinkle the cucumber with salt and leave for 30 minutes.

2. Crack the legs and claws off the crab. Remove the meat from the claws and legs, but leave four thin legs whole as a garnish.

3. Separate the underbody from the shell. Remove and discard the stomach sac and the gray, feathered gills.

4. Scrape the brown meat from the shell and crack open the underbody. Use a skewer to pick out the meat.

5. Rinse the cucumber, drain well and squeeze out excess moisture. Mix together the cucumber, crab meat and ginger.

6. Arrange the Chinese cabbage on serving plates, to represent crab shells. Pile equal quantities of crab mixture onto the Chinese cabbage, leaving some of the leaf showing. Garnish with a whole crab leg and some grated, pickled ginger, if you can get it.

7. Mix together the vinegar, sherry and soy sauce. Serve in little bowls with the crab.

TIME Preparation takes about 30 minutes.

SERVING IDEAS A rice or pasta salad would be excellent with this dish.

SHRIMP AND CASHEWS IN PINEAPPLE WITH TARRAGON DRESSING

Served in the pineapple shells, this impressive salad is ideal for a summer lunch.

SERVES 4

---

2 small fresh pineapples, with green tops
1¼ cups cooked, peeled shrimp
1 cup roasted, unsalted cashew nuts
2 celery stalks, thinly sliced
4 tbsps lemon juice
1 egg
2 tbsps superfine sugar
1 tbsp tarragon vinegar
2 tsps chopped fresh tarragon or 1 tsp dried
½ cup heavy cream

---

1. Cut the pineapples carefully in half lengthwise, leaving their green tops attached.

2. Cut out the pineapple flesh carefully, leaving a ¼ inch border of flesh on the inside of the shell. Remove the cores and cut the flesh into bite-sized pieces.

3. Put the chopped pineapple into a bowl, along with the shrimp, cashew nuts and celery. Pour in the lemon juice and mix well. Divide the mixture equally between the pineapple shells, and chill them in the refrigerator.

4. In a heat-proof bowl, whisk together the egg and sugar. Stand the bowl over a pan of simmering water, and whisk in the vinegar and tarragon. Continue whisking until the mixture has thickened.

5. Remove the bowl from the heat and allow to cool completely, whisking occasionally.

6. When completely cold, whip the cream until it is just beginning to thicken, then fold it into the dressing mixture.

7. Pour the cream dressing over the salad in the pineapple shells and serve.

TIME Preparation takes about 30 minutes, cooking takes about 10-15 minutes.

SPANISH RICE AND SOLE SALAD

A complete meal in itself, this salad is ideal for a summer lunch.

SERVES 4

2 large lemon sole, each filleted into 4
 pieces
4-6 peppercorns
Slice of onion
1 tbsp lemon juice
¾ cup long grain rice
1 small eggplant
2 tbsps olive oil
1 red pepper, seeded and chopped into ¼
 inch dice
1 shallot, finely chopped
1 green pepper, seeded and chopped into
 ¼ inch dice
3 tbsps Italian dressing
1 tbsp chopped fresh mixed herbs or ½ tsp
 dried
1 cup mayonnaise
1 clove garlic, crushed
1 tsp tomato paste
1 tsp paprika
Salt and pepper
2 bunches watercress, to garnish

1. Lay the sole fillets in an ovenproof dish, together with the peppercorns, slice of onion, lemon juice and just enough water to cover. Sprinkle with a little salt and cover the dish with foil or a lid. Poach in a preheated oven, 350°F, for 8-10 minutes. Allow the fish to cool in the liquid, then cut each fillet into 1 inch pieces.

2. Cook the rice in boiling water until soft. Rinse in cold water and separate the grains with a fork.

3. Cut the eggplant in half and sprinkle with 2 tsps salt. Allow to stand for half an hour, then rinse very thoroughly. Pat dry and cut into ½ inch dice.

4. Heat the oil in a large frying pan, and fry the eggplant, until it is soft. Allow the eggplant to cool, then mix it into the rice along with the shallot, peppers, half the chopped herbs and the Italian dressing.

5. Mix together the mayonnaise, garlic, tomato paste, paprika, remaining herbs and seasoning.

6. Arrange the rice on one side of a serving dish and the sole pieces on the other. Spoon the mayonnaise over the sole and garnish the dish with watercress.

TIME Preparation will take about 20 minutes, cooking takes about 15-20 minutes.

SOLE AND MUSHROOM TURNOVERS

These delicious individual pies make a warming family lunch or supper dish.

SERVES 4

4 sole fillets, skinned
Salt and pepper
½ cup milk
1 cup mushrooms, trimmed and thinly
    sliced
2 tbsps butter
Juice of 1 lemon
5 tbsps white bread crumbs mixed with
    1 tbsp crushed hazelnuts
3 tbsps hazelnut, or lemon stuffing mix
12 oz puff pastry
Beaten egg, for glazing
Poppy seeds, for sprinkling

1. Season the sole fillets and roll them up jelly roll fashion. Secure each roll with a wooden pick and poach gently in the milk for about 10 minutes in a preheated oven, 350°F.

2. Drain the fish and allow it to cool. Remove the wooden picks.

3. Put the mushrooms and butter in a saucepan with the lemon juice. Cook over a moderate heat for about 5 minutes.

4. Allow the mushrooms to cool and then stir in the bread crumb mix.

5. Roll out the pastry, quite thinly, into 4 circles, each 6 inches in diameter. Brush the edges with beaten egg.

6. Put a fish roll into the center of each circle and top with a quarter of the mushroom mixture. Pull the pastry edges up and over the fish and pinch together to seal.

7. Preheat the oven to 400°F. Place the turnovers on a greased cookie sheet and glaze with the beaten egg. Sprinkle with a few poppy seeds.

8. Bake in the pre-heated oven for about 25 minutes, or until well risen, puffed and golden. Serve piping hot.

TIME Preparation will take about 25 minutes, plus the cooling time, cooking will take about 35 minutes.

MONKFISH AND PEPPER KEBABS

Monkfish is ideal for making kebabs as it can be cut into firm cubes which do not disintegrate during cooking.

SERVES 4

8 slices of bacon
1 lb monkfish, skinned and cut into 1 inch
   pieces
1 small green pepper, seeded and cut into
   1 inch pieces
1 small red pepper, seeded and cut into
   1 inch pieces
12 small mushroom caps
8 bay leaves
3 tbsps vegetable oil
½ cup dry white wine
4 tbsps tarragon vinegar
2 shallots, finely chopped
1 tbsp fresh tarragon, chopped
1 tbsp fresh chervil or parsley, chopped or
   ½ tsp dried
1 cup butter, softened
Salt and freshly ground black pepper

1. Cut the bacon slices in half lengthwise and then again in half crosswise.

2. Put a piece of the fish onto each piece of bacon and roll the bacon around the fish.

3. Thread the bacon and fish rolls onto large skewers, alternating them with pieces of pepper, the mushrooms and the bay leaves.

4. Brush the kebabs with oil and arrange on a broiler pan.

5. Preheat the broiler. Place the kebabs 3 inches from the heat and broil for 10-15 minutes, turning them frequently to prevent the kebabs from burning.

6. Heat the white wine, vinegar and shallots in a small saucepan until boiling. Cook rapidly to reduce by half.

7. Add the herbs and lower the heat.

8. Using a fork or small whisk beat the butter bit by bit into the hot wine mixture, whisking rapidly until the sauce becomes thick. Season to taste.

9. Arrange the kebabs on a serving plate and serve with a little of the sauce spooned over and the remainder in a separate jug.

TIME Preparation takes 30 minutes, cooking takes about 25 minutes.

PIZZA MARINARA

Seafood pizzas are wonderful – this one is especially tasty.

SERVES 4

¾ cup all-purpose flour, sifted
1 tsp baking powder
½ tsp salt
⅓ cup milk
2 tbsps salad oil
4 oz canned tomatoes
1 tsp tomato paste
1 clove crushed garlic
½ tsp dried oregano
½ tsp dried basil
Pinch of fennel seeds
Salt and pepper
¾ cup shrimp
4 anchovy fillets
8-10 mussels
1 tsp capers
2-3 black olives
4 oz sliced mozzarella cheese

1. Sift the flour, baking powder and salt into a bowl and add milk and oil. Stir vigorously until mixture leaves the sides of the bowl.

2. Press it into a ball and knead it in the bowl for about 2 minutes until smooth. Cover, and leave it to sit while preparing sauce.

3. Put the tomatoes, paste, herbs, seasoning and garlic together in a small saucepan. Bring to a boil and reduce to thicken. Leave to cool.

4. Roll out the pizza dough into a 12-inch circle. Spread the sauce evenly leaving a ½ inch border around the edge. Scatter over the shellfish, anchovy fillets, olives and capers.

5. Slice the cheese thinly and place it on top of the fish.

6. Bake in a 425°F oven for 10-15 minutes until cheese browns lightly and the crust is crisp.

TIME Preparation takes 15 minutes, cooking takes 25-30 minutes.

Broiled Herring with Dill and Mustard

Mustard and dill enhance the fish perfectly in this dish.

SERVES 4

---

4 tbsps fresh dill, chopped
6 tbsps mild mustard
2 tbsps lemon juice, or white wine
4-8 fresh herrings, cleaned but heads and
  tails left on
2 tbsps butter or margarine, melted
Salt and pepper

---

1. Mix the dill, mustard and lemon juice or wine together thoroughly.

2. Cut three slits, just piercing the skin, on both sides of each herring and lay them on a broiler pan.

3. Spread half the mustard mixture equally over the exposed side of each fish, pushing some into the cuts.

4. Preheat the broiler. Spoon a little of the melted butter over each herring, and broil the fish 3-5 inches from the heat for 5-6 minutes.

5. Turn the fish over and spread the remaining mustard and dill mixture over them. Spoon over the remaining melted butter and broil for another 5-6 minutes.

6. Sprinkle the fish with a little salt and pepper before serving.

TIME Preparation takes about 10 minutes, cooking takes 12-15 minutes, although this may be longer if the herring are large.

SERVING IDEAS Arrange the fish on a serving dish, garnished with lemon wedges and sprigs of fresh dill. Serve with new potatoes, if available.

MONKFISH IN PAPRIKA SAUCE

Monkfish is a firm, succulent fish, which should be used more often than it is. It is ideal for use in kebabs or fish casseroles, and in this recipe it is complemented magnificently by the creamy paprika sauce.

SERVES 4

1 lb monkfish fillets

Lemon juice

1 bay leaf

Slice of onion

6 peppercorns

2 tbsps butter

1 cup mushrooms, trimmed and sliced

1 small red pepper, seeded and sliced

1 shallot, finely chopped

2 tsps paprika

1 clove garlic, crushed

¼ cup all-purpose flour

1¼ cups milk

1 tbsp fresh parsley, chopped or ½ tbsp dried

1 tsp fresh thyme, chopped or ½ tsp dried

1 tsp tomato paste

Salt and pepper

8 oz fresh pasta, cooked

2 tbsps sour cream, or plain yogurt

1. Cut the monkfish into 1 inch chunks. Put these into an ovenproof dish with the lemon juice, bay leaf, onion, peppercorns and just enough water to cover. Cover with a lid and poach for about 10 minutes in a preheated oven at 350°F.

2. Melt the butter in a saucepan and stir in the mushrooms, pepper, shallot, paprika and garlic. Cook gently, until the pepper begins to soften.

3. Stir the flour into the mushrooms and pepper. Gradually add the milk, stirring until the sauce has thickened.

4. Remove the fish from the dish and strain off the liquid. Stir enough of this liquid into the sauce to make it of coating consistency. Add the parsley, thyme and tomato paste to the sauce and simmer for 2-3 minutes. Season to taste.

5. Arrange the hot, cooked pasta on a serving plate and place the fish on top. Coat with the paprika sauce, and spoon over the sour cream, or yogurt, to serve.

TIME Preparation takes about 20 minutes, and cooking takes about 16 minutes.

VARIATIONS Use any other firm-fleshed white fish instead of the monkfish.

SERVING IDEAS A mixed salad would be ideal to serve with this dish.

RED SNAPPER WITH HERB & MUSHROOM SAUCE

This fish has a slight taste of shrimp. It is often cooked with the liver left in – a delicacy.

SERVES 4

1 lb small mushrooms, left whole

1 clove garlic, finely chopped

3 tbsps olive oil

Juice of 1 lemon

1 tbsp fresh parsley, finely chopped or 1 tbsp dried

2 tsps fresh basil, finely chopped or ½ tsp dried

1 tsp fresh marjoram or sage, finely chopped or ½ tsp dried

4 tbsps dry white wine mixed with ½ tsp cornstarch

Anchovy paste

4 red snapper, each weighing about 8 oz

2 tsps white bread crumbs

2 tsps freshly grated Parmesan cheese

1. Heat the olive oil in a small frying pan and add the mushrooms and garlic. Cook over moderate heat for about 1 minute, until the garlic and mushrooms are slightly softened. Add all the herbs, lemon juice and white wine and cornstarch mixture. Bring to a boil and cook until thickened. Add anchovy essence to taste. Set aside while preparing the fish.

2. To clean the fish, cut along the stomach from the gills to the vent, the small hole near the tail. Clean out the cavity of the fish, leaving the liver, if desired.

3. To remove the gills, lift the flap and snip them out with a sharp pair of scissors. Rinse the fish well and pat dry.

4. Place the fish head to tail in a shallow ovenproof dish that can be used for serving. The fish should fit snugly into the dish.

5. Pour the prepared sauce over the fish and sprinkle with the bread crumbs and Parmesan cheese.

6. Cover the dish loosely with foil and bake in a preheated oven, 375°F, for about 20 minutes. Uncover for the last 5 minutes, if desired, and raise the oven temperature slightly. This will lightly brown the fish.

TIME Preparation takes about 30 minutes, cooking takes about 5 minutes for the sauce and 20 minutes for the fish.

COOK'S TIP If you don't want to clean the fish yourself, buy them ready-cleaned.

STUFFED SOLE

This traditional German dish is elegant enough for a formal dinner party.

SERVES 6

4 tbsps butter or margarine

2 tbsps flour

1½ cups fish or vegetable stock

1 cup button mushrooms, sliced

6 oz peeled, cooked shrimp

4 oz canned, frozen or fresh cooked
    crabmeat

4 tbsps heavy cream

2 tbsps brandy

1 oz fresh bread crumbs

Salt and pepper

6-12 sole fillets, depending upon size

4 tbsps melted butter

1. Preheat the oven to 350°F. Melt 4 tbsps butter and add the flour. Cook for about 3 minutes over gentle heat or until pale straw colored. Add the stock and bring to a boil. Add the mushrooms and allow to cook until the sauce thickens.

2. Add the cream and re-boil the sauce. Remove the sauce from the heat and add the brandy, shrimp, crab and bread crumbs.

3. Skin the sole fillets and spread the filling on the skinned side. Roll up and arrange in a buttered baking dish. Spoon melted butter over the top and cook in the pre-heated oven for 20-30 minutes, until the fish is just firm.

TIME Preparation takes about 30 minutes, cooking takes 20-30 minutes.

VARIATIONS For special occasions, substitute lobster for the crabmeat.

SERVING IDEAS Serve with a green vegetable such as broccoli, asparagus or spinach. Accompany with new potatoes tossed in parsley butter.

SARDINE AND TOMATO GRATIN

Fresh sardines are becoming more widely available and this recipe makes the most of these delicious fish.

SERVES 4

3 tbsps olive oil

2 lbs large fresh sardines, descaled and cleaned

2 leeks, cleaned and sliced

½ cup dry white wine

6-8 tomatoes, skinned and quartered

Salt and pepper

2 tbsps fresh basil, chopped, or 1 tbsp dried basil

2 tbsps fresh parsley, chopped

½ cup Parmesan cheese, grated

½ cup dry bread crumbs

1. Heat the oil in a frying pan and fry the sardines until they are brown on both sides. It may be necessary to do this in several batches, to prevent the fish from breaking up.

2. When all the sardines are cooked, set them aside and cook the leeks gently in the sardine oil. When the leeks are soft, pour in the wine and boil rapidly, until it is reduced by about two thirds.

3. Add the tomatoes, seasoning and herbs to the leeks and cook for about 1 minute. Pour the vegetables into an ovenproof dish and lay the sardines on top.

4. Sprinkle the cheese and bread crumbs evenly over the sardines and bake in a preheated oven, 425°F, for about 5 minutes.

TIME Preparation takes about 20-25 minutes, cooking takes about 15 minutes.

VARIATIONS Try substituting herrings or mackerel for the sardines. They will take a little longer to fry.

SERVING IDEAS Cut a few anchovy fillets in half lengthwise and arrange them in a lattice on top of the gratinée, before serving with hot garlic bread.

SWEET-SOUR FISH

In China this dish is almost always prepared with freshwater fish, but sea bass is also an excellent choice.

SERVES 2

1 sea bass, snapper or carp, weighing about 2 lbs, cleaned

1 tbsp dry sherry

Few slices fresh ginger

½ cup sugar

6 tbsps cider vinegar

1 tbsp soy sauce

2 tbsps cornstarch

1 clove garlic, crushed

2 green onions, shredded

1 small carrot, peeled and finely shredded

½ cup bamboo shoots, shredded

1. Rinse the fish well inside and out. Make three diagonal cuts on each side of the fish with a sharp knife.

2. Trim off the fins, leaving the dorsal fin on top.

3. Trim the tail to two neat points.

4. In a wok, bring enough water to a boil to cover the fish. Gently lower the fish into the boiling water and add the sherry and ginger. Cover the wok tightly and remove at once from the heat. Allow to stand 15-20 minutes to let the fish cook in the residual heat.

5. To test if the fish is cooked, pull the dorsal fin – if it comes off easily the fish is done. If not, return the wok to the heat and bring to a boil. Remove from the heat and leave the fish to stand a further 5 minutes. Transfer the fish to a heated serving dish and keep it warm. Take all but 4 tbsps of the fish cooking liquid from the wok. Add the remaining ingredients including the vegetables and cook, stirring constantly, until the sauce thickens. Spoon some of the sauce over the fish to serve and serve the rest separately.

TIME Preparation takes about 25 minutes, cooking takes about 15-25 minutes.

COOK'S TIP The diagonal cuts in the side of the fish ensure even cooking.

SWORDFISH FLORENTINE

*Swordfish has an almost "meaty" texture. Here it has a distinctly
Mediterranean flavor.*

SERVES 4

---

4 swordfish steaks, about 6-8 oz each in
  weight
Salt, pepper and lemon juice
Olive oil
2 lbs fresh spinach, stems removed and
  leaves well washed

Garlic Mayonnaise
2 egg yolks
1-2 cloves garlic
Salt, pepper and dry mustard
Pinch cayenne pepper
1 cup olive oil
Lemon juice or white wine vinegar

---

1. Sprinkle fish with pepper, lemon juice
and olive oil. Place under a preheated
broiler and broil for about 3-4 minutes per
side. Fish may aso be cooked on an
outdoor barbecue grill.

2. Meanwhile, use a sharp knife to shred
the spinach finely. Place in a large
saucepan and add a pinch of salt. Cover
and cook over moderate heat with only the
water that clings to the leaves after
washing. Cook about 2 minutes, or until
leaves are just slightly wilted. Set aside.

3. Place egg yolks in a food processor or
blender. Add the garlic. Process several
times to mix eggs and purée garlic. Add
salt, pepper, mustard and cayenne pepper.
With the machine running, pour oil through
the funnel in a thin, steady stream.

4. When the sauce becomes very thick, add
enough lemon juice or vinegar to thin
slightly.

5. To serve, place a bed of spinach on a
plate and top with the swordfish. Spoon
some of the garlic mayonnaise on top of the
fish and serve the rest separately.

TIME Preparation takes about 25 minutes, cooking takes about 6-8 minutes.

PREPARATION The garlic mayonnaise may be prepared in advance and will
keep for 5-7 days in the refrigerator. It is also delicious served with poached
shellfish, chicken or vegetables. If too thick, thin the sauce with hot water.

HALIBUT AND CRAB HOLLANDAISE

Rich and creamy, the hollandaise sauce adds an air of sophistication to this lovely dish.

SERVES 4

4 large fillets of halibut
1 bay leaf
Slice of onion
5 tbsps white wine
2 egg yolks
1 tbsp lemon juice
Pinch cayenne pepper
Pinch paprika
½ cup butter, melted
1 tbsp butter
2 tbsps flour
2 tbsps heavy cream
Salt and pepper
8 oz crab meat

1. Put the fish with the bay leaf, onion slice, wine and just enough water to cover the fish, into a baking dish. Cover and cook in a preheated oven, 325°F, for 10 minutes.

2. Put the egg yolks, lemon juice, cayenne and paprika into a blender, or food processor. Turn the machine on and gradually pour in the melted butter. Continue processing, until the hollandaise sauce is thick. Set aside.

3. Put the 1 tbsp unmelted butter into a saucepan, melt over a gentle heat and stir in the flour. Cook gently for 1 minute.

4. Remove the fish from the baking dish and strain the cooking liquid onto the flour and butter in the saucepan, stirring well to prevent lumps from forming. Cook this sauce gently, until it is smooth and has thickened. Stir in the cream, but do not allow to boil. Season to taste.

5. Stir the crab meat into the fish stock sauce and pour this mixture into a flameproof dish. Lay the halibut fillets on top and cover these with the hollandaise sauce.

6. Brown the sauce under the broiler before serving.

TIME Preparation will take about 15 minutes and cooking takes about 20 minutes.

SERVING IDEAS Serve with new potatoes and broccoli.

TROUT MEUNIÈRE AUX HERBES

The miller (meunier) caught trout fresh from the mill stream and his wife used the flour that was on hand to dredge them with, or so the story goes.

SERVES 4

4 even-sized trout, clean and trimmed
Flour
Salt and pepper
½ cup butter
Juice of 1 lemon
2 tbsps chopped fresh herbs such as
    parsley, chervil, tarragon, thyme or
    marjoram
Lemon wedges to garnish

1. Trim the trout tails to make them more pointed. Rinse the trout well.

2. Dredge the trout with flour and shake off the excess. Season with salt and pepper. Heat half the butter in a very large frying pan and, when foaming, place in the trout. It may be necessary to cook the trout in two batches to avoid overcrowding the pan.

3. Cook over fairly high heat on both sides to brown evenly. Depending on size, the trout should take 5-8 minutes per side to cook. The dorsal fins will pull out easily when the trout are cooked. Remove the trout to a serving dish and keep them warm.

4. Wipe out the pan and add the remaining butter. Cook over moderate heat until beginning to brown, then add the lemon juice and herbs. When the lemon juice is added, the butter will bubble up and sizzle. Pour immediately over the fish and serve with lemon wedges.

TIME Preparation takes 15-20 minutes, cooking takes 5-8 minutes per side for the fish and about 5 minutes to brown the butter.

SERVING IDEAS Serve with new potatoes and peeled, cubed cucumber quickly sautéed in butter and chopped dill.

SINGAPORE FISH

The cuisine of Singapore was much influenced by that of China. In turn, the Chinese welcomed ingredients from Singapore like curry powder into their own cuisine.

SERVES 6

1 lb whitefish fillets

1 egg white

1 tbsp cornstarch

2 tsps white wine

Salt and pepper

Oil for frying

1 large onion, cut into ½ inch thick wedges

1 tbsp mild curry powder

1 small can pineapple chunks, drained and juice reserved, or ½ fresh pineapple, peeled and cubed

1 small can mandarin orange segments, drained and juice reserved

1 small can sliced water chestnuts, drained

1 tbsp cornstarch mixed with juice of 1 lime

2 tsps sugar (optional)

1. Starting at the tail end of the fillets, skin them using a sharp knife.

2. Slide the knife back and forth along the length of each fillet, pushing the fish flesh along as you go.

3. Cut the fish into even-sized pieces, about 2 inches.

4. Mix together the egg white, cornstarch, wine, salt and pepper. Place the fish in the mixture and leave to stand while heating the oil in a wok.

5. When the oil is hot, fry a few pieces of fish at a time until light golden brown and crisp. Remove the fish and put on paper towels to drain. Continue until all the fish is cooked.

6. Remove all but 1 tbsp of the oil from the wok and add the onion. Stir-fry the onion for 1-2 minutes and add the curry powder. Cook the onion and curry powder for another 1-2 minutes. Add the juice from the pineapple and mandarin oranges and bring to a boil.

7. Combine the cornstarch and lime juice and add a tablespoon of the boiling fruit juice. Return the mixture to the wok and cook until thickened, about 2 minutes. Taste and add sugar if desired. Add the fruit, water chestnuts and fried fish to the wok and stir to coat. Heat through 1 minute and serve immediately.

TIME Preparation takes about 25 minutes, cooking takes about 10 minutes.

Kung Pao Shrimp with Cashew Nuts

It is said that Kung Pao invented this dish, but to this day no one knows who he was!

SERVES 6

½ tsp fresh ginger, chopped

1 tsp garlic, chopped

1½ tbsps cornstarch

¼ tsp baking soda

Salt and pepper

¼ tsp sugar

1 lb uncooked shrimp

4 tbsps oil

1 small onion, diced

1 large or 2 small zucchini, cut into ½ inch cubes

1 small red pepper, cut into ½ inch cubes

½ cup cashew nuts

Sauce

¾ cup chicken stock

1 tbsp cornstarch

2 tsps chili sauce

2 tsps bean paste (optional)

2 tsps sesame oil

1 tbsp dry sherry or rice wine

1. Mix together the ginger, garlic, cornstarch, baking soda, salt, pepper and sugar.

2. If the shrimp are unpeeled, remove the peels and the dark vein running along the rounded side. If large, cut in half. Place in the dry ingredients and leave to stand for 20 minutes.

3. Heat the oil in a wok and when hot add the shrimp. Cook, stirring over high heat for about 20 seconds, or just until the shrimp change color. Transfer to a plate.

4. Add the onion to the same oil in the wok and cook for about 1 minute. Add the zucchini and red pepper and cook for about 30 seconds.

5. Mix the sauce ingredients together and add to the wok. Cook, stirring constantly, until the sauce is slightly thickened. Add the shrimp and the cashew nuts and heat through completely.

TIME Preparation takes about 20 minutes, cooking takes about 3 minutes.

STUFFED FISH

A whole baked fish makes an impressive main course for a dinner party. The stuffing makes the fish go further and with no bones it's easy to serve and eat.

SERVES 4-6

2-3 lb whole fish such as carp or sea bass
Salt and pepper
2 tbsps melted butter

Stuffing

1 tbsp butter or margarine
1 small onion, finely chopped
1½ cups mushrooms, coarsely chopped
1 hard-cooked egg, peeled and coarsely
    chopped
¾ cup fresh bread crumbs, white or whole-
    wheat
Pinch salt and pepper
2 tsps fresh dill, chopped
2 tsps fresh parsley, chopped
Pinch nutmeg

Sauce

½ cup sour cream
Pinch sugar
Grated rind and juice of ½ lemon
Pinch salt and white pepper
Lemon slices and parsley sprigs to garnish

1. Ask the assistant to gut and bone the fish for you, leaving on the head and tail. Sprinkle the cavity of the fish with salt and pepper and set it aside while preparing the stuffing.

2. To chop the onion finely, peel it and cut it in half lengthwise. Place the onion cut side down on a chopping board. Using a large, sharp knife, make four cuts into the onion, parallel to the chopping board, but not completely through to the root end. Using the pointed tip of the knife, make four or five cuts into the onion lengthwise, following the natural lines in the onion and not cutting through to the root end. Next, cut the onion crosswise into thin or thick slices as desired and the onion should fall apart into individual dice. Keep fingers well out of the way when slicing.

3. Melt the butter or margarine in a medium-sized saucepan and add the chopped onion and mushrooms. Cook briefly to soften the vegetables and take off the heat. Stir in the remaining stuffing ingredients.

4. Spread the stuffing evenly into the cavity of the fish, sprinkle the top with melted butter and place the fish in lightly buttered foil in a large baking dish. Bake in a preheated 350°F oven for about 40 minutes, basting frequently.

5. When the fish is cooked, combine the sauce ingredients and pour over the fish. Cook another 5 minutes to heat the sauce, but do not allow it to bubble. Remove the fish to a serving dish and garnish with lemon and parsley.

TIME Preparation takes about 20 minutes. If boning the fish yourself, add a further 30 minutes. Cooking takes approximately 45 minutes.

COOK'S TIP Cover the head and tail of the fish with lightly greased foil about halfway through cooking time. This will prevent the fish from drying out and improve the appearance of the finished dish.

361

PAELLA

This dish has as many variations as Spain has cooks! Fish, meat and poultry combine with vegetables and rice to make a complete meal.

SERVES 6

12 mussels in their shells

6 clams

Flour

6 oz cod, skinned and cut into 2 inch pieces

12 large shrimp

3 chorizos or other spicy sausage

3 tbsps oil

2 lb chicken, cut in 12 serving-size pieces

1 small onion, chopped

1 clove garlic, crushed

2 small peppers, red and green, seeded and shredded

3 cups long grain rice

Large pinch saffron

Salt and pepper

4 cups boiling water

4 oz frozen peas

3 tomatoes, peeled, seeded and chopped or shredded

1. Scrub the clams and mussels well to remove beards and barnacles. Discard any with broken shells or those that do not close when tapped. Leave the mussels and clams to soak in water with a handful of flour for 30 minutes.

2. Remove the heads and legs from the shrimp, if desired, but leave on the tail shells.

3. Place the sausage in a saucepan and cover with water. Bring to a boil and then simmer for 5 minutes. Drain and slice into ¼ inch rounds. Set aside.

4. Heat the oil and fry the chicken pieces, browning evenly on both sides. Remove and drain on paper towels.

5. Add the sausage, onions, garlic and peppers to the oil in the frying pan and fry briskly for about 3 minutes.

6. Combine the sausage mixture with uncooked rice and saffron and place in a special paella dish or a large oven- and flame-proof casserole. Pour on the water, season with salt and pepper and bring to a boil. Stir occasionally and allow to boil for about 2 minutes.

7. Add the chicken pieces and place in a preheated 400°F oven for about 15 minutes.

8. Add the clams, mussels, shrimp, cod and peas and bake another 10-15 minutes or until the rice is tender, chicken is cooked and mussels and clams open. Discard any that do not open. Add the tomatoes 5 minutes before the end of cooking time and serve immediately.

TIME Preparation takes about 30-40 minutes, cooking takes about 35-40 minutes.

Sole with Spicy Tomato Sauce

This delicious recipe mixes white fish with a spicy Mexican sauce.

SERVES 4

3 oz cream cheese
1 tsp dried oregano
Pinch cayenne pepper
4 whole fillets of sole
Lime slices and dill to garnish

Tomato Sauce

1 tbsp oil
1 small onion, chopped
1 celery stalk, chopped
1 chili pepper, seeded and chopped
¼ tsp each ground cumin, coriander and
    ginger
½ red and ½ green pepper, seeded and
    chopped
14 oz can tomatoes
1 tbsp tomato paste
Salt, pepper and a pinch sugar

1. Heat the oil in a heavy-based pan and cook the onion, celery, chili pepper and spices for about 5 minutes over very low heat.

2. Add red and green peppers and the remaining ingredients and bring to a boil. Reduce heat and simmer for 15-20 minutes, stirring occasionally. Set aside while preparing the fish.

3. Mix the cream cheese, oregano and cayenne pepper together and set aside.

4. Skin the fillets using a filleting knife. Start at the tail end and hold the knife at a slight angle to the skin.

5. Push the knife along using a sawing motion, with the blade against the skin. Dip fingers in salt to make it easier to hold onto the fish skin. Gradually separate the fish from the skin.

6. Spread the cheese filling on all 4 fillets and roll each up. Secure with wooden picks.

7. Place the fillets in a lightly greased baking dish, cover and bake for 10 minutes in a preheated 350°F oven.

8. Pour over the tomato sauce and bake another 10-15 minutes. Fish is cooked when it feels firm and looks opaque. Garnish with lime slices and dill.

TIME Preparation takes about 30 minutes and cooking takes 20-25 minutes.

SERVING IDEAS Add rice and an avocado salad.

SMOKED HADDOCK AND EGG QUICHE

This classic quiche is a firm favorite for lunches and suppers alike.

SERVES 6

8 oz ready-made whole-wheat dough
12 oz smoked haddock fillet
½ cup chicken stock
2 hard-cooked eggs, chopped
1 tbsp fresh chives, chopped
¾ cup Cheddar cheese, grated
3 eggs
1 cup milk
Salt and pepper

1. Roll out the pastry to fit a 9 inch deep fluted pie pan. Press the edges up well and push the base well down. Prick the base with a fork and bake for 15 minutes in a preheated oven, 375°F.

2. Place the fish in a saucepan and poach gently in the chicken stock for about 8 minutes, or until just tender. Drain the fish and flake it into a bowl, discarding any skin or bones.

3. Mix the chopped eggs, chives and cheese into the fish, and spread this mixture evenly into the part-baked pastry shell.

4. Beat together the eggs and milk, and season to taste. Pour over the fish mixture in the pastry shell.

5. Bake at 375°F for 25-30 minutes, or until the filling is set.

TIME Preparation will take about 25 minutes, and cooking takes about 40 minutes.

CHILLED FISH CURRY

This sophisticated, mild curry will serve four as a refreshing summer lunch, or eight as an elegant appetizer.

SERVES 4-8

8 oz fresh salmon fillet
12 oz whitefish fillet
Chicken stock
Salt and pepper
½ cup mayonnaise
1½ cups plain yogurt
2 tsps curry powder
Juice and grated rind of ½ lemon
¾ cup peeled shrimp

Garnish
Kiwi fruit, peeled and sliced
Sprigs fresh mint
Shredded coconut

1. Put the salmon and whitefish fillets into a shallow pan and add just enough chicken stock to cover.

2. Season to taste and simmer gently, until the fish is just tender.

3. Remove the fish carefully from the cooking liquid and leave to cool slightly.

4. In a medium-sized bowl, mix together the mayonnaise and the yogurt. Blend in the curry powder and the lemon juice and rind.

5. Flake the cooked fish, removing any bones and skin. Mix the flaked fish and the shrimp into the curry sauce.

6. Arrange the fish curry on serving plates and garnish with slices of kiwi fruit, sprigs of fresh mint and coconut.

TIME Preparation takes about 20 minutes, and cooking takes about 6 minutes.

VARIATIONS If you prefer, use slices of peeled cucumber instead of the kiwi fruit.

RAINBOW TROUT WITH SPINACH AND WALNUT STUFFING

SERVES 6-8

---

1 fresh whole rainbow trout, weighing
   2½ lbs, cleaned and boned
2 lbs fresh spinach
1 small onion
¼ cup polyunsaturated margarine
⅓ cup walnuts, coarsely chopped
4 oz fresh white bread crumbs
1 tbsp fresh parsley, chopped or ½ tsp dried
1 tbsp fresh thyme, chopped or ½ tsp dried
¼ grated nutmeg
Salt and freshly ground black pepper
Juice of 2 lemons
Watercress sprigs and lemon slices, to garnish

---

1. If you cannot buy the fish boned, remove the bone yourself. Carefully cut the underside of the fish from the end of the slit made when the fish was cleaned, to the tip of the tail.

2. Place the fish, belly side down, on a flat work surface, spreading the cut underside out to balance the fish more easily.

3. Using the palm of your hand press down along the backbone of the fish, pushing the spine downwards towards the work surface.

4. Turn the fish over and using a sharp knife, carefully pull the backbone away from the fish, cutting it away with scissors at the base of the head and tail.

5. Remove the backbone completely and pull out any loose bones you may find with a pair of tweezers. Lay the boned fish in the center of a large square of lightly oiled aluminum foil and set aside.

6. Wash the spinach leaves well and tear off any coarse stalks. Put the spinach into a large saucepan and sprinkle with salt. Do not add any extra water. Cover and cook over a moderate heat for about 3 minutes.

7. Turn the spinach into a colander and drain well, pressing with the back of a wooden spoon to remove all the excess moisture.

8. Chop the cooked spinach very finely using a sharp knife.

9. Peel and chop the onion finely and fry gently in about 1 tbsp of the margarine until soft, but not colored.

10. Stir the cooked onion into the chopped spinach along with the walnuts, bread crumbs, herbs, nutmeg, salt, pepper and half of the lemon juice. Mix well to blend evenly.

11. Use the spinach stuffing to fill the cavity inside the trout. Push the stuffing in firmly, re-shaping the fish as you do so. Allow a little of the stuffing to show between the cut edge of the fish.

12. Seal the foil over the top of the fish, but do not wrap it too tightly.

13. Place the fish in a roasting pan and bake in a preheated oven at 350°F for 35 minutes.

14. Carefully unwrap the fish and transfer it to a large serving dish.

15. Using a sharp knife, peel away the skin from all exposed sides of the fish. If possible remove some skin from the underside also.

16. While the fish is still hot, dot with the remaining margarine, sprinkle with the remaining lemon juice, then serve garnished with the watercress and sliced lemon.

TIME Preparation takes 35-40 minutes, cooking takes about 40 minutes.

SZECHUAN FISH

The piquant spiciness of Szechuan pepper is quite different from that of black or white pepper. Beware, though, too much can numb the mouth temporarily!

SERVES 6

Whole chili peppers
1 lb whitefish fillets
Pinch salt and pepper
1 egg
5 tbsps flour
6 tbsps white wine
Flour for dredging
Oil for frying
2 oz cooked ham, cut in small dice
1 inch piece fresh ginger, finely diced
½-1 red or green chili pepper, cored,
    seeded and finely diced
6 water chestnuts, finely diced
4 green onions, finely chopped
3 tbsps light soy sauce
1 tsp cider vinegar or rice wine vinegar
½ tsp ground Szechuan pepper (optional)
1¼ cups light fish stock
1 tbsp cornstarch dissolved with 2 tbsps
    water
2 tsps sugar

1. To prepare the garnish, choose unblemished chili peppers with the stems on. Using a small, sharp knife, cut the peppers in strips, starting from the pointed end.

2. Cut down to within ½ inch of the stem end. Rinse out the seeds under cold running water and place the peppers in iced water.

3. Leave the peppers to soak for at least 4 hours or overnight until they open up like flowers.

4. Cut the fish fillets into 2 inch pieces and season with salt and pepper. Beat the egg well and add flour and wine to make a batter. Dredge the fish lightly with flour and then dip into the batter. Mix the fish well.

5. Heat a wok and when hot, add enough oil to deep-fry the fish. When the oil is hot, fry a few pieces of fish at a time, until golden brown. Drain and proceed until all the fish is cooked.

6. Remove all but 1 tbsp of oil from the wok and add the ham, ginger, diced chili pepper, water chestnuts and green onions. Cook for about 1 minute and add the soy sauce and vinegar. If using Szechuan pepper, add at this point. Stir well and cook for another 1 minute. Remove the vegetables from the pan and set them aside.

7. Add the stock to the wok and bring to a boil. When boiling, add 1 spoonful of the hot stock to the cornstarch mixture. Add the mixture back to the stock and reboil, stirring constantly until thickened.

8. Stir in the sugar and return the fish and vegetables to the sauce. Heat through for 30 seconds and serve at once.

TIME Preparation takes about 30 minutes. Chili pepper garnish takes at least 4 hours to soak. Cooking takes about 10 minutes.

FISH MILANESE

These fish, cooked in the style of Milan, have a crispy crumb coating and the fresh tang of lemon juice.

SERVES 4

8 sole fillets
2 tbsps dry vermouth
1 bay leaf
6 tbsps olive oil
Seasoned flour for dredging
2 eggs, lightly beaten
Dry bread crumbs
Oil for shallow frying
6 tbsps butter
1 clove garlic, crushed
2 tsps parsley, chopped
2 tbsps capers
1 tsp fresh oregano, chopped
Juice of 1 lemon
Lemon wedges and parsley to garnish

1. Skin the fillets with a sharp filleting knife. Remove any small bones and place the fillets in a large, shallow dish. Combine the vermouth, oil and bay leaf in a small saucepan and heat gently. Allow to cool completely and pour over the fish. Leave the fish to marinate for about 1 hour turning them occasionally.

2. Remove the fish from the marinade and dredge lightly with the seasoned flour.

3. Dip the fillets into the beaten eggs to coat, or use a pastry brush to brush the eggs onto the fillets. Dip the egg-coated fillet into the bread crumbs, pressing the crumbs on firmly.

4. Heat the oil in a large frying pan. Add the fillets and cook slowly, about 3 minutes, on both sides until golden brown. Remove and drain on paper towels.

5. Pour the oil out of the frying pan and wipe it clean. Add the butter and the garlic and cook until both turn a light brown. Add the herbs, capers and lemon juice and pour immediately over the fish. Garnish with lemon wedges and sprigs of parsley.

TIME Preparation takes 1 hour for the fish to marinate, cooking takes about 6 minutes. It may be necessary to cook the fish in several batches, depending upon the size of the frying pan.

HERRING WITH APPLES

The addition of fresh tasting apples beautifully complements the delicious and wholesome flavor of herring.

SERVES 4

---

4 herrings, cleaned
2 large apples
1 large onion, peeled and thinly sliced
4 large potatoes, peeled and sliced
Salt and freshly ground black pepper
½ cup apple cider
2 oz dried bread crumbs
¼ cup polyunsaturated margarine
1 tbsp fresh parsley, chopped

---

1. Cut the heads and tails from the herrings and split them open from the underside.

2. Put the herring, belly side down, on a flat surface and carefully press along the back of each fish with the palm of your hand, pushing the backbone down towards the surface.

3. Turn the herring over and with a sharp knife, carefully prise away the backbone, pulling out any loose bones as you go. Do not cut the fish into separate fillets. Wash and dry them well.

4. Peel, quarter, core and slice one of the apples.

5. Lightly grease a shallow baking pan and layer with the potatoes, apple and onions, seasoning well with salt and pepper between layers.

6. Pour the apple cider over the layers and cover the dish with foil. Bake in a preheated oven 350°F for 40 minutes.

7. Remove the dish from the oven and arrange the herring fillets over the top.

8. Sprinkle the bread crumbs over the herrings and dot with half of the margarine.

9. Increase the oven temperature to 400°F and return the dish to the oven for about 10-15 minutes, or until the herrings are cooked and brown.

10. Core the remaining apple and slice into rounds, leaving the peel on.

11. Melt the remaining margarine in a frying pan and gently fry the apple slices.

12. Remove the herrings from the oven and garnish with the fried apple slices and chopped parsley. Serve at once.

TIME Preparation takes 15-20 minutes, cooking takes about 50 minutes.

COOK'S TIP If you do not want to bone the fish yourself, buy boned fish.

SEA BASS WITH VEGETABLES

A delicious lemon sauce perfectly enhances the fish in this impressive dish.

SERVES 4

1 sea bass, weighing 2-2½ lbs
8 oz broccoli or green beans
1 lb new potatoes
4 zucchini
4 very small turnips
1 small bunch green onions
2 carrots
¼ cup butter
¼ cup flour
1¼ cups milk
1 small bunch fresh thyme or 1 tbsp dried
3 lemons
Paprika
Fresh parsley, chopped
Salt and pepper

1. Clean the bass, trim the fins, but leave the head and tail on. Put salt and pepper and half thyme inside the fish. Put the fish in the center of a large square of buttered foil. Add the juice of 1 lemon, wrap fish loosely, and bake at 350°F for 40-60 minutes, depending on weight.

2. Cut the broccoli into small florets (or trim the beans, but leave whole). Scrub potatoes and turnips but do not peel. Cut the zucchini into 2-inch strips. Trim the green onions, leaving some of the green. Peel the carrots, and cut to the same size as the zucchini.

3. Keeping the vegetables in separate piles, steam the potatoes and turnips for 15-20 minutes, the carrots, broccoli or beans for 6 minutes, and the zucchini and green onions for 3 minutes. Arrange on a serving dish and keep warm.

4. Remove the fish from its wrapping and place in the middle of the vegetables; keep them warm while preparing the sauce.

5. Melt the butter, add the flour and cook gently for 1-2 minutes until pale brown. Stir in the milk, add the flour gradually, stirring constantly. Bring the sauce to boil for 1-2 minutes until thick. Strain in the cooking liquid from the fish.

6. Peel and segment the remaining lemons, working over a bowl to collect any juice. Chop the remaining thyme and add to the sauce along with lemon segments and juice.

7. Sprinkle paprika on the potatoes, and chopped parsley on the carrots. Coat the fish with lemon sauce and serve.

TIME Preparation takes 30 minutes, cooking takes 40-60 minutes.

My Favorite Recipes

My Favorite Recipes

_____

_____

_____

_____

_____

_____

_____

_____

_____

_____

_____

_____

_____

_____

_____

_____

_____

_____

_____

_____

_____

_____

_____

_____

_____

_____

INDEX

CONVERSION TABLE

VOLUME MEASUREMENT (dry)

1/8 teaspoon = .5 mL
1/4 teaspoon = 1 mL
1/2 teaspoon = 2 mL
3/4 teaspoon = 4 mL
1 teaspoon = 5 mL
1 tablespoon = 15 mL
2 tablespoons = 25 mL
1/4 cup = 50 mL
1/3 cup = 75 mL
2/3 cup = 150 mL
3/4 cup = 175 mL
1 cup = 250 mL
2 cup = 1 pint = 500 mL
3 cups = 750 mL
4 cups = (1 quart) = 1 L

VOLUME MEASUREMENT (fluid)

1 fluid ounce (2 tablespoons) = 30 mL
4 fluid ounces (1/2 cup) = 125 mL
8 fluid ounces (1 cup) = 250 mL
12 fluid ounces (1 1/2 cups) = 375 mL
16 fluid ounces (2 cups) = 500 mL

DIMENSION

1/16 inch = 2 mm
1/8 inch = 3 mm
1/4 inch = 6 mm
1/2 inch = 1.5 cm
3/4 inch = 2 cm
1 inch = 2.5 cm

TEMPERATURES

250° F = 120° C
275° F = 140° C
300° F = 150° C
325° F = 160° C
350° F = 180° C
375° F = 190° C
400° F = 200° C
425° F = 220° C
450° F = 230° C

WEIGHT

1/2 ounce = 15 g
1 ounce = 30 g
3 ounces = 85 g
3.75 ounces = 100 g
4 ounces = 115 g
8 ounces = 225 g
12 ounces = 340 g
16 ounces = (1 pound) = 450 g

SUGAR

1 teaspoon = 4 g
1 tablespoon = 12 g
4 tablespoons (1/4 cup) = 50 g
5 1/3 tablespoons (1/3 cup) = 70 g
1/2 cup = 100 g
2/3 cup = 135 g
3/4 cup = 150 g
1 cup = 200 g